OSPREY
MILITARY

CAM

YARMUK 636AD

GENERAL EDITOR DAVID G. CHANDLER

OSPREY MILITARY

CAMPAIGN SERIES 31

YARMUK 636AD

THE MUSLIM CONQUEST OF SYRIA

DAVID NICOLLE

◄ *The Wadi al 'Ali from the site of the destroyed Syrian village of al 'Al. This stood at a very narrow part of the Golan plateau where the head of the Wadi al 'Ali gorge running westwards almost reached the head of another gorge running south-east into the Wadi Ruqqad. As such it was a naturally defensible position, where the Byzantine commander almost certainly established his main camp before the battle of Yarmuk. (Author's photograph)*

FOR A CATALOGUE OF ALL BOOKS PUBLISHED
BY OSPREY MILITARY, AUTOMOTIVE
AND AVIATION PLEASE WRITE TO:

The Marketing Manager, Osprey Direct USA,
PO Box 130, Sterling Heights, MI 48311-0130, USA.
Email: info@ospreydirectusa.com

The Marketing Manager, Osprey Direct UK,
PO Box 140, Wellingborough, Northants, NN8 4ZA,
United Kingdom.
Email: info@ospreydirect.co.uk

VISIT OSPREY AT
www.ospreypublishing.com

First published in Great Britain in
1994 by Osprey Publishing, Elms Court,
Chapel Way, Botley, Oxford OX2 9LP,
United Kingdom
Email: info@ospreypublishing.com

© 1994 Osprey Publishing Ltd.
Reprinted 2000

ISBN 1-85532-414-8
Printed in China through World Print Ltd.
Produced by DAG Publications Ltd
for Osprey Publishing Ltd.
Colour bird's eye view illustrations by
Peter Harper.
Cartography by Micromap.
Wargaming Yarmuk by Ian Drury
Mono camerawork by M&E
Reproductions, North Fambridge,
Essex.

CONTENTS

◀ *The area of the battle of Ajnadayn is a sparsely populated part of modern Israel. The old Arab villages north of the battlefield, through which the defeated Byzantines fled, are all abandoned. Only this mysterious ruined 'Tomb of the Prophet Paul' watches over some scattered Israeli fields. (Author's photograph)*

The Middle East in 634

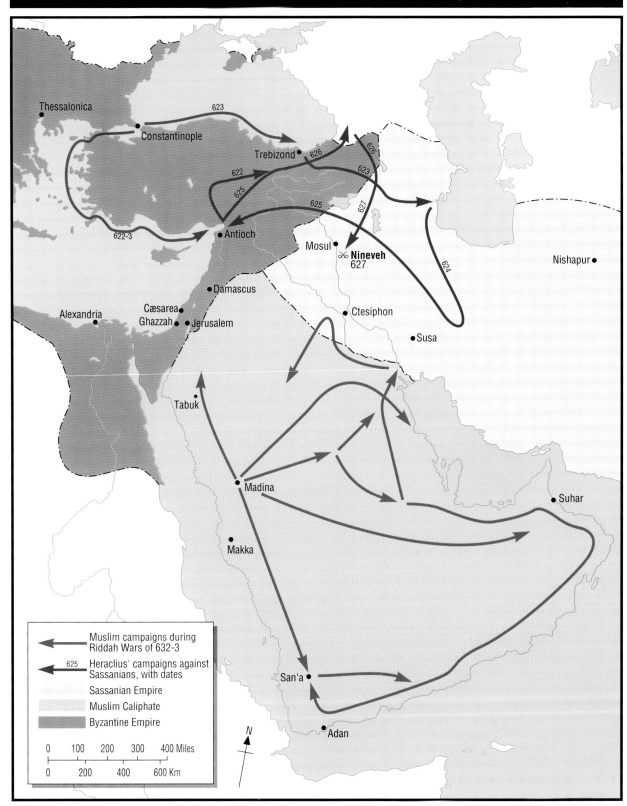

Thessalonica

Constantinople
623

Trebizond
626
626
622
623
625
625
627
624

Antioch
Mosul
✂ **Nineveh**
627
Nishapur

Damascus
622-3

Alexandria
Cæsarea
Ghazzah
Jerusalem
Ctesiphon
Susa

Tabuk

Madina
Suhar

Makka

San'a

Adan

Muslim campaigns during
Riddah Wars of 632-3

625 Heraclius' campaigns against
Sassanians, with dates

Sassanian Empire

Muslim Caliphate

Byzantine Empire

0   100   200   300   400 Miles

0   200   400   600 Km

N

ORIGINS OF THE CAMPAIGN

The battle of Yarmuk in 636 was a turning point in history. If the Byzantines had won, Graeco-Roman domination of the Middle East could have continued and medieval Europe might have been denied the cultural contacts with eastern Asia that Islamic civilization opened up.

Yet the whole process of 7th century Muslim Arab expansion remains little understood outside a small circle of specialists. Few contemporary accounts survive, although there are highly detailed descriptions dating from a generation or so later. It is also difficult to separate fact from pious myth. Today, however, the 'pendulum of credibility' has swung back from the almost total disbelief of early 20th century Western historians to what might be described as a 'twilight of historical reality'.

Byzantine Syria: the Arena of Conflict

A great deal is known about Syria in the last decades of Byzantine rule. As now, it consisted of three distinct zones – a westward-looking Mediterranean coast, a rich agricultural hinterland and a much larger region of semi-desert. The coast was largely Greek speaking; Syriac and Aramaean speaking Semitic peoples inhabited the agricultural zone; while the semi-desert steppes were already Arab. Big cities were dominated by Greek speakers, though their citizens were as mixed as the country itself, with large Jewish populations plus groups of Georgians and Armenians as well as Latin-speaking Europeans. Use of the Greek language did not, however, prove a sense of identity with the Byzantine Empire and the effectiveness of Byzantine rule in this remarkably complex region is open to doubt.

▼ *The fortifications of Umm al Rasas, a deserted city in southern Jordan known in Byzantine times as Kastron Mefaa. It was one of the first Syrian cities to fall to the Muslim Arabs and continued to flourish into the 9th century. (Author's photograph)*

7

North of the Yarmuk river (modern-day Syria and Lebanon), Byzantine local government and defence werc based upon cities, some of which had existed for thousands of years. Southern Syria and what are now Jordan, Israel and the occupied territories of Palestine included huge Byzantine Imperial estates as well as flourishing cities and church lands. Syria also had a very military appearance, all cities being strongly walled and some having large permanent garrisons. In the north these faced the threat of Persian invasion, while in the south any political disruption could encourage raiding by bedouin tribes.

Syria, along with much of the rest of the Byzantine Empire, had suffered a series of blows since the mid-6th century: earthquakes, plagues, economic decline, Sassanian Persian invasions and a generation of Sassanian occupation. Worst of all were earthquakes and plagues. A series of epidemics starting in 540 cut the population by a third in the towns infested with plague-carrying rats. Meanwhile the tented nomads escaped virtually unscathed. There was, in fact, a large Arab-speaking population within Byzantine Syria, many being Christian while others were Jewish or pagan.

Natural features and man-made communications played a vital role in the Muslim Arab conquest of Syria. In the north, mountains were the only real barriers, running parallel to the coast and then eastwards along the Anatolian foothills. In the centre and south deep valleys cut through the plateau. All ran east–west except for the north–south Jordan and Biqa'a valleys. Emesa (Hims) was the most important communications and military centre in Byzantine north-central Syria, Caesarea Maritima (Qaysariya) being the main defensive base in Palestine. The Roman road system was still in reasonable repair, yet it still took several days to get infantry from Caesarea to Gaza (Ghazzah). Cavalry, who were now the most important part of the army, moved faster by riding on cleared areas on each side of the paved Roman roads. The most important such road ran from Egypt to Damascus. North of al Lajjun in Palestine

▼ *Among many mosaics in Jordan are these stylized views of fortified towns dating from around 650, a few years after the battle of Yarmuk. Each* *town has a defensive wall with towers and a church, usually with a dome. (Museum store, Mt. Nebo, Jordan; author's photograph)*

▶ *The aqueduct of ancient Caesarea Maritima on the Mediterranean coast of Palestine brought water from north of the city. Caesarea was the main Byzantine military base as well as being a vital port on the otherwise bleak southern coast. (Author's photograph)*

this split into two, one branch continuing across the Golan plateau, the other taking a less direct route along the upper Jordan valley to meet the main road from Tyre to Damascus, or crossing the Jordan to rejoin the first road on the Golan.

Despite a thousand years of alien Greek and Roman rule, Syria still retained its own distinctive Semitic culture. This was particularly apparent in religion. In addition to non-Christian minorities, the bulk of the population in some provinces belonged to churches regarded as heretical elsewhere in the Empire. Palestine was largely Orthodox Christian, but central and northern Syria were Monophysite – a theological difference that meant a very great deal in those days! The deeply anti-Jewish Orthodox Church hierarchy regarded Syria as a hotbed of 'Judaizers, Jewish-Christians and Jews'. In return the large Jewish minority had little love for its Orthodox rulers, particularly after the Emperor Heraclius decreed that all Jews must convert to Christianity in 630. But the most alienated community was that of the Samaritans

▶ *Fragment of 7th century carved ivory; provincial Byzantine workmanship from a Lombardic tomb at Nocera Umbra in Italy. A cavalryman in a crested helmet with a long neck-guard wears a scale or mail cuirass. He does not use stirrups. (Mus. dell'Alto Medio Evo, Rome)*

◀ *Umm al Jimal, an almost deserted 'dead city' on the edge of the desert in northern Jordan, was probably controlled by the Christian Arab Ghassanids in Byzantine times. This tower in what is popularly called the 'barracks' is decorated with Christian crosses. It was built around AD 412 and includes two early examples of machicolations from which rocks could be dropped on an attacker. (Author's photograph)*

▼ *Left and right: The story of 'David and Goliath' on a sequence of 6th century Coptic Egyptian reliefs. On the left Saul is flanked by guardsmen, one with a spear and shield, the other with a shield and a sword hung from a baldric. On the right Goliath is portrayed twice, on both occasions wearing scale or stylized mail armour and a large helmet. (Coptic Mus., Cairo; author's photographs)*

who, persecuted by Christians and Jews alike, had risen in support of the Sassanian Persian invaders and would soon help the Muslim Arabs. Paganism would survive in Syria for another century and a half under Muslim rule. The ancient *Maiumas* 'water festival' was still held at Gerasa (Jarash) as late as 535, though the old orgies involving dancing girls and public nude bathing had been toned down and given a new Christian guise.

During the Sassanian Persian invasion of the Byzantine Empire the old Byzantine army collapsed and a new Emperor, Heraclius, had to rebuild it from shattered fragments. This he did with remarkable success. Ironically, he set out on his epic reconquest of the Middle East in the same year, 622, that an obscure Arab religious leader fled from his home town of Makka to seek sanctuary in the neighbouring town of Yathrib (later to be known as Madina). That year of 622 would become year 1 AH in a new Muslim calender, the year in which the Prophet Muhammad made his *Hijra* or escape to set up the new religious community of *Muslims*.

The early 7th century was also a time of quickening military change in the Byzantine Empire after centuries of stagnation, and Byzantium was certainly not in a state of collapse when it faced the new challenge from Arabia. On the other hand, the Byzantine army was unprepared for an attack from such an unexpected direction.

The Arabs: the Neglected Neighbours

The Arabic-speaking peoples of the Arabian peninsula and neighbouring areas followed many religions and different ways of life. Some lived in towns as merchants or craftsmen, but most were *fallahin* peasant farmers in the oases of Arabia, the fertile hills of Yemen or the villages of Byzantine Syria and Sassanian Iraq. Even among the nomads there were important distinctions between the camel-raising true *badw* (bedouin) of the deep desert, the sheep- and camel-raising *swayih* of the grassy steppes, and the *ra'w* semi-nomads on the fringes of the cultivated zone. Recent research shows that there were plenty of small villages or farms well beyond the Romano-Byzantine frontier in what are now Syria and Jordan. Nor were Arab nomads ever excluded from the settled areas, while the degree of conflict between nomad and farmer has been greatly exaggerated, often for modern political reasons. Within the desert, tribes normally migrated across each other's territory by peaceful agreement rather than constantly fighting each other.

One technological development had an immense impact on the balance of power in the steppes and desert. This was the wood-framed North Arabian camel saddle, which was secured on top of the animal's hump – the older so-called South Arabian

saddle lacked a frame and was placed behind the hump. Though adequate for peaceful purposes, the old type was no use in war. Once the richer camel-raising tribes adopted the new saddle it became very difficult for neighbouring empires to control the tribes. Both Byzantium and Sassanian Persia came to rely on Arab allies to control the desert, and in Byzantine Syria the last of these allies were the Ghassanids. To the Byzantines these Ghassanids were mere frontier auxiliaries, but within Arabia they were often seen as great kings. Their tribal leader or *shaykh* was called the *Strategos Parembolon* 'Commander of nomad auxiliaries' by Byzantium, the Arab *hira* or encampment being called a *Parembole* in Greek. The Ghassanid federation of pro-Byzantine tribes was shattered by the Sassanian conquest and had not yet been rebuilt when the Muslim Arabs erupted on to the scene.

Meanwhile the Ghassanids were by no means the only Christian Arab tribe. For many years Byzantium had insisted that tribes become Christian in return for Byzantine support. In Arabia itself wandering monks spread the Gospel by preaching at annual tribal fairs. Muhammad himself was a native of the Hijaz, and there were Christian monasteries in the north of this area serving as centres of Byzantine influence. More monks also

▲ *The Syrian and Arabian deserts were not a vast empty area into which Muslim Arab armies could retreat at will. Many parts, particularly the* **harra** *or lava plains, are still virtually impassable even to nomadic bedouin. Such areas of shattered volcanic rock covering hundreds of square miles exist in Arabia, Syria, Iraq and, as here, in Jordan. (Author's photograph)*

sought refuge among the Christian Arab tribes during the Sassanian invasion of Palestine. Christianity was similarly spreading in Yemen to the south. Even in Oman, in eastern Arabia, Christianity had been recorded since the 4th century. Most of the people of present-day Iraq may also have been Christian by the early 7th century.

Despite the spread of Christianity among the Arabs, the Byzantines still looked upon their desert neighbours as barbarians, set apart by their nomadic way of life, and the Greeks had little real knowledge of the Arabian peninsula. Their image of the Arabs was stuck in an outdated mould, describing them as 'wild untamed beasts', 'beastly and barbarous enemies', the Old Testament 'hosts of Midian' or as agents of Divine Wrath. At first, Christians did not realize that Islam was a new religion, seeing it as just another Judeo-Christian heresy.

▲*The parched Wadi 'Araba valley, south of the Dead Sea, separates southern Palestine from ancient Moab, now* *southern Jordan. The Muslims used the tiny oasis of Gharandal in the Wadi 'Araba as a base. (Author's photograph)*

Within Arabia there had, of course, been many other changes. The northern Arab peoples had learned much from both Byzantines and Sassanians, particularly in warfare, and they could face the troops of these neighbouring empires on equal terms. To the south, Yemeni society was headed by an aristocracy of *kabir* clan chiefs, *qail* princes, and the military *satraps* who governed the country following its conquest by the Sassanian Persians. This was a relatively rich area, but the lucrative incense trade had virtually ceased since the Romano-Byzantine Empire had become Christian. Nevertheless, Meccan merchant families, like the Quraysh who dominated the city until the coming of Islam, were prosperous and owned property within Byzantine-ruled Syria.

On the other hand, there were many times when Sassanian Persian influence was stronger than that of Byzantium, and from their capital at Ctesiphon (more correctly Tyspwn in Middle Persian) the Sassanian Emperors encouraged their own Arab allies, the Lakhmids, to bring Arabia within the Persian orbit. By the mid-6th century Lakhmid-Sassanian control may theoretically have reached Najran in northern Yemen, while in Oman local *shaykhs* known as the Julanda ruled as Lakhmid-Sassanian clients. The Sassanians' defeat by the Emperor Heraclius of Byzantium undermined their power within Arabia, and in the period of near anarchy that followed a great deal of weaponry fell into the hands of other Arab tribes. Meanwhile Makka gradually emerged as a new power centre.

The Coming of Islam

Into this fluid political and religious situation came the Prophet Muhammad who started to preach the new faith of Islam.* Muhammad's mission and his rise to political power coincided with the Sassanian occupation of Syria. While the reconquering Byzantines rebuilt a confederation of allied tribes to the north, Muhammad attracted Arab tribes to Islam in the Hijaz. The rulers of Yemen to the south, Bahrayn on the Gulf coast and Oman in the east also accepted Islam in recognition of the new

---

* It is important to note that, for Muslims, Islam is not a 'new faith'; it is the first religion given by God to Adam. For Muslims, Muhammad merely brought back the original True Faith to a misguided world.

A Muslim élite soldier equipped for infantry warfare. His iron and bronze helmet comes from Iraq and is of a Central Asian type which would become very common in the following centuries. He also wears two dir' mail hauberks with an Arab durra'a tunic between them. The use of a baldric rather than a waist-belt to carry his sword is also typically Arab. The yellow cloth around this man's head and shoulders suggests that he was one of the Ansar, the first men to help the Prophet Muhammad back in Arabia. (Angus McBride)

▶ Top and Bottom: Among the finest 6th-7th century Coptic carved ivories are a series of panels illustrating the story of Joseph on the 'Throne of Archbishop Maximian', made around AD 550. They show bedouin Arab warriors as well as Byzantine troops. In the top picture the child Joseph is sold in Egypt. Both bedouin have long plaited hair and are dressed in the simple izzar wrap-around cloth still worn by Muslims while on Haj or pilgrimage. Bottom shows Joseph, now governor of Egypt, guarded by soldiers in typical Byzantine military uniforms. (Cathedral Museum, Ravenna; author's photographs)

throughout the peninsula. The Emperor in Constantinople, meanwhile, seems to have been blissfully unaware of what was happening south of Syria.

Muhammad at first regarded Christians as allies. Only after his followers clashed with pro-Byzantine Arab tribesmen at Mu'ta in 629 did the two religions become rivals. A year later the Muslims made a peace treaty with the bishop of Aila (modern 'Aqabah) and various south Jordanian tribes. This area still lay outside Byzantine control for, after defeating the Sassanians, the Emperor Heraclius set up a new defence line from Ghazzah on the Mediterranean to the southern end of the Dead Sea, leaving the deep south outside the Empire. The new line was only designed to protect communications from bandits, and the bulk of Byzantine defences were concentrated in northern Syria, facing the traditional Sassanian foe. But this new defence line meant that raiders from Arabia could now go around the Gulf of 'Aqabah into Egypt or north towards Ghazzah before meeting regular Byzantine troops.

After the Prophet Muhammad died in 632 he was succeeded politically, though not in a religious sense, by a Caliph (Khalifah) or 'viceregent', the first of whom was Abu Bakr. Very soon Abu Bakr realized that if the Muslims did not control the tribes then the Byzantines would, and raids were launched to impose Muslim authority on all Arabic-speaking peoples. As yet, Muhammad's religious message applied only to pagan Arabs rather than to Christians and Jews who, as 'Peoples of the Book', already worshipped the One True God. But these early Muslim raids aimed in the Ghazzah area soon

dominance of Muslim Makka and Madina. The Riddah Wars, which erupted immediately after the Prophet's death, were partly an attempt by these areas to regain their independence, partly an effort by Muslims from Makka and Madina to extend their control over Arabia. They resulted in the consolidation of a powerful new Muslim state

brought Muslim troops into confrontation with Byzantine soldiers. In 634 the Muslims defeated a Byzantine force, killing its commander who as a *Candidatos* ranked as a member of the Emperor's own bodyguard. The following year's earthquake and the appearance of a sword-shaped comet apparently coming from the south would later be interpreted as omens of the forthcoming Muslim conquest.

To the east, beyond the Byzantine frontier, the Muslims were consolidating their authority among the tribes of the Syrian steppes. Here the transition to a new government seems to have been peaceful. Gradually the frontier regions were also taken over.

The Muslim conquest of the Balqa region of central Jordan was strategically important, for it was from here that the Muslims would launch their invasion of Syria and Palestine. For once, desert invaders and a settled empire – in this case the Muslim Arabs and the Byzantines – were evenly matched, perhaps more so than they ever would be again.

▼ *Roman roads criss-cross much of the Middle East, but few are still in such remarkable condition as this stretch between Antioch and Qinnasrin (ancient Chalcis). Such roads played a vital part in Byzantine strategic planning, and even the highly mobile Muslim Arab armies used them. (Author's photograph)*

THE OPPOSING LEADERS

The Byzantine Commanders

It is normal for more to be known about victors than vanquished, but the information is particularly unbalanced where the battle of Yarmuk is concerned. The only well documented Byzantine figure is Heraclius himself. He was a courageous though tragic figure, the first Emperor to lead his armies in person for many generations. Heraclius adopted the Greek title of *Basileos* in 629, thus claiming to rule by Divine Right, finally shedding the Roman titles used by previous Emperors . His propagandists portrayed Byzantium's wars in a very religious light, using that most potent of Christian relics, the Wood of the Holy Cross, to inspire the fighting fervour of his troops. Parallels were also made between Heraclius's early victories and those of the Old Testament Jews. The Emperor's biographer, George of Pisidia, even used Heraclius's marriage problems to draw a parallel between the Byzantine Emperor and the ancient King David.

Heraclius's reputation clearly worried the Muslims in the early stages. Yet the historical record shows that, though he was a capable general, he was anxious and prone to doubt. He did know the geography of Syria personally but tended to interfere with the daily conduct of operations and was not good at delegating responsibility. By the time of the Muslim invasion of Syria Heraclius was also a sick man, suffering from hydrophobia and dropsy (probably cancer). His greatest military achievement was to have regained the Byzantine provinces lost since the reign of the Emperor Maurice. His tragedy was to have then lost an even greater area to the rising power of Islam.

Little is known about Heraclius's brother Theodore, the *kouropalates* or senior officer who commanded Byzantine forces at Ajnadayn. He was a political enemy of the Emperor's new wife Martina, but was also an experienced general, having fought several campaigns against Sassanian armies in the east. Muslim chroniclers portray him as aggressive, foolhardy and ignoring the Emperor's instructions to await reinforcements. Various eastern Christian sources also blame him for the Byzantine débâcle. After Ajnadayn, Heraclius was clearly angry with his brother, either for his failure or for fleeing the field, and sent him back to the capital.

Even less is known about Theodore Trithourios, who commanded the Byzantine armies that attempted to drive the Muslim invaders from Syria in 636 and who was defeated at Yarmuk. He was the Byzantine *Sakellarios*, or Treasurer, which suggests that the Emperor was worried about the problem of paying his troops and thus maintaining their morale. He may still have been the *Magister Militum per Orientem* 'Master of the Eastern Soldiers' and is believed to have been a eunuch.

Vahan, the Byzantine field commander at Yarmuk, was of Armenian origin, and he probably knew the Middle East better than the newcomer Theodore Trithourios. As commander of the main base at Emesa, Vahan would have been second only to the Emperor in the military hierarchy of Byzantine Syria. He may then have been put in charge of fresh troops sent from his own homeland of Armenia and from the capital, Constantinople (Istanbul), as well as local Arab forces.

Niketas, another senior Byzantine officer at Yarmuk, had a particularly interesting background. He was the son of the famous Sassanian Persian general Shahrbaraz, who had led various Sassanian armies in Syria. Thus Niketas may have known the area well. Shahrbaraz met Heraclius four years later and got Byzantine support for his own attempt to become Sassanian Emperor – in which he succeeded for a brief period. Shahrbaraz is said to have been sympathetic to Christianity, and his son Niketas was almost certainly a Christian. Almost nothing is known about the troops Niketas commanded,

Early Islamic sources describe turbans as the 'crown of the Arabs', but these were not the tightly wound bulky turbans seen in later centuries. Instead they were little more than headcloths. Here a member of the early Muslim Arab military élite has the fully mail armour characteristic of rich tribesmen and is armed with the spear and shield similarly of Arab troops. (Angus McBride)

▲ *The most famous pieces of early 7th century Byzantine metalwork are the 'David Plates', found at Lampousa in Cyprus and probably made to celebrate the Emperor Heraclius's victory over the Sassanian Persians – before his catastrophic defeats by the Muslims. The largest plate illustrates the battle between David and Goliath. On the left are two Israelite warriors*

though there were still Persian units in Syria, either unable or unwilling to go home following the recent Sassanian defeat. Niketas's loyalty to Byzantium may have been shallow, as some sources suggest he attempted to go over to the Muslims after the battle of Yarmuk.

Rather more is known about Jabala, the last 'king' of the Ghassanids, perhaps because he was a Christian Arab well remembered by his Muslim Arab foes. For a quarter of a century Jabala had

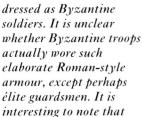

dressed as Byzantine soldiers. It is unclear whether Byzantine troops actually wore such elaborate Roman-style armour, except perhaps élite guardsmen. It is interesting to note that *their helmets are covered with decorative caps, one corner of the leading figure's helmet still being visible beneath this cover. Goliath at the centre is dressed in Romano-Byzantine style though* *his shield has a lion's head boss identical to a 4th century Sassanian shield-boss now in the British Museum. On the right two Philistine warriors again have Romano-Byzantine mail* *armour, but their helmets are very different and reflect those worn by late Sassanian troops. (Met. Museum of Art, New York; author's photographs)*

fought hard against Byzantium's Sassanian enemies. He survived the battle of Yarmuk and for a time made peace with the new Muslim rulers of Syria. But then Jabala quarrelled with the Caliph 'Umar and left for Byzantine territory, taking many of his fighting men with him. He eventually settled in the strategic frontier area of Charsionon (Cappadocia) in central Anatolia where his descendants and their followers proved their worth against future Muslim raids. They lost their Arab language but never their

pride in their origins. A later Byzantine Emperor, Nicephorus (802–11), was himself descended from Jabala the Ghassanid.

The Muslim Commanders

A great deal was recorded about the men who led the Muslim Arab conquest of Syria, their deeds, characters and individual foibles, but it is almost impossible to separate fact from fiction.

'Umar, the second Caliph of Islam, was respected rather than loved. He was a man of exceptional moral strength, high intelligence and great political skill. Though autocratic, he remained humble in his dress and private life. Muslim expansion began under his predecessor, Abu Bakr, but 'Umar then directed the greatest period of conquest, controlling his military leaders by his own power of command.

'Umar also laid the foundations for a regularly organized and paid Muslim army with the *Diwan* military list, a register of all men eligible for military stipends. On the one hand 'Umar founded several new *amsar* military centres, some of which developed into great cities. On the other he ensured that horses captured in Syria, one of the ancient world's main horse-breeding areas, were systematically collected before every new military operation, since the first Muslim armies were acutely short of cavalry.

Khalid Ibn al Walid was a very different man and had once been one of the Prophet Muhammad's most effective military opponents. Impetuous, fearless, occasionally unscrupulous, a lover of money and not very religious, Khalid was nevertheless one of the greatest tacticians in military history. He was known as the 'Sword of God' (but in Arabic, that most subtle of languages, this implies that Khalid was merely a weapon to be wielded by greater men). Although Khalid had shown a streak of brutality during the Riddah Wars within Arabia, he may later have been the first Muslim leader to impose the relatively light *jizyah* tax on enemies who surrendered voluntarily, using this money to pay his troops.

Abu 'Ubaida could hardly have been more different to the fearsome Khalid. Pious but lacking military skill, Abu 'Ubaida was nevertheless a man of considerable common sense. 'Umar probably put him in charge of the invading Muslim Arab armies in Syria for political reasons, describing him as 'the faithful guardian of the people'. He had been much

▼ *Qasr al Hallabat; a fortress in the Jordanian desert, which originally formed part of the Roman limes (frontier defences). The Byzantines turned it into a monastery and the Muslim Umayyads transformed it into a 'desert palace'. (Author's photograph)*

more conciliatory than Khalid towards those ex-Riddah War rebels who now served in Muslim forces. Relations with the defeated Christians in Syria were also much easier after Abu 'Ubaida took command.

'Amr Ibn al As was again a man of different character, generally being considered a subtle politician as well as an excellent military commander. He led the Muslim conquest of south-western Palestine, though 'Amr's greatest achievement came later with his conquest of Byzantine Egypt. Like many other military leaders, he then fell from favour, retiring to his hard-won estates in Palestine.

▶ *The most famous and complete series of wall-paintings from the early Islamic period are in the isolated reception hall and* **Hamam** *bath-house at Qusayr 'Amra in the Jordanian desert. They date from around 740. This standing figure with a long tunic and a sword hanging from a baldric is remarkably similar to illustrations of the first Umayyad Caliphs on Islamic coins. He probably represents a member of the ruling élite. (in situ, Qusayr 'Amra, Jordan, author's photograph)*

▼ *The tomb of Khalid Ibn al Walid, the real commander of the Muslim forces at the battle of Yarmuk, in the Great Mosque at Hims. This was completely rebuilt in Seljuk Turkish style shortly before the First World War. (Author's photograph)*

THE OPPOSING ARMIES

Byzantine Recruitment

The Roman citizen army was a thing of the past, and the new Byzantine army was a mercenary force. By the 6th century there were three forms of recruitment: local volunteers plus 'barbarian' foreigners either individually enlisted as *foideratoi* or in ethnic units as *symmachoi*. The Emperor Maurice had recently tightened up on the quality of equipment with annual roll-calls to check that units were up to strength. There had been an increase in internal recruitment, and, during his wars against the Sassanians, Heraclius reintroduced the concept of hereditary military service. Nevertheless, it took time, money and the disruption of local economies to raise new forces, so the Byzantines found it easier to recruit Arab auxiliaries or warlike, if traditionally unreliable, Armenians. An official 'alliance' with the Empire gave Arab tribal leaders status among the other tribes, particularly if their *shaykh* was awarded the title of *Patricius*, or *Bitriq* in Arabic. Unfortunately, the financial rewards that went with this status did not always appear on time, as the Byzantine Empire was now desperately short of cash. Other foreigners included 'allied' Armenians, captured Persians, Turco-Hun nomads from the Ukraine and Germanic Lombards from Italy.

Most of the light cavalry came from such external 'allies' or specialist warlike groups within the Empire, but the ordinary infantry tended to be recruited internally. They were recruited in Illyria (Albania) and Thrace in the Balkans, Isauria, Pontus and Cappadocia in what is now Turkey. In addition to Orthodox and 'heretical' Christians, the army included Jews, pagans, and Manichaeans (followers of a 'dualist' faith which would later reappear in western Europe as the Albigensians). Not surprisingly, many Byzantine commanders spent a lot of time worrying about religious tensions within the ranks!

◀ *The most realistic illustration of early Byzantine armour is on the 'Isola Rizza Dish', found in northern Italy and dating from the late 6th or early 7th centuries. The horseman wears a plumed segmented helmet and a short-sleeved lamellar cuirass, and he rides without stirrups. (Castelvecchio Museum, Verona; author's photograph)*

Having lost its independence in the 5th century, Armenia was occupied by Byzantine and Sassanian garrisons. An indigenous military aristocracy consisted of a higher nobility of *Ishkhans* and lesser barons known as *Nakharars*. Each noble had his own military following of *Azatani* minor aristocrats and *Sepouh* freemen, normally equipped as cavalry. Their military reputation was very high, and Armenian troops had become increasingly important to the Byzantine army. *Nakharars* were encouraged to settle in western Anatolia and European Thrace, while in the east Heraclius recognized David Saharouni as a quasi-independent Armenian princeling in return for Saharouni's help against the Muslims.

By the late 6th century there was not much difference in status between various Byzantine units. Nevertheless the *Optimates* did form a cavalry élite. They appear to have been recruited from the best of the old Gotho-Graeci, descendants of Ostrogoths who settled inside the empire after being driven from Italy by invading Lombards. Based in Bythnia in north-western Anatolia, they formed a corps of heavy cavalry equipped in the Germanic manner. In Syria, ex-Sassanian Persian troops formed part of the garrisons at Heliopolis (Ba'albakk) and Emesa (Hims) but most of the troops within Syria seem to have been of Arab origin. Many towns appear to have had a *Hira* or encampment of semi-settled bedouin next door serving as a local defence force.

The Organization of Byzantine Armies

The Byzantine army clung to its Roman traditions of organization and discipline. The philosophy of separating civil and military authority, though sometimes abandoned in times of danger, was also designed to give army leaders a free hand. In contrast, a concentration of power in the hands of the Emperor led to a widespread 'psychology of dependence' which had a profound impact on military initiative.

Beneath the Emperor himself a *Magister Militum per Orientem* commanded all troops in the eastern part of the Empire. The basic administrative and tactical unit was the *tagma*, theoretically consisting of 300 men. Ten *tagmatas* formed a *meros* (regiment), which could also be divided into three *moera*, while three *meros* formed an army. Though the terminology was complex there was clearly a coherent command structure during the 6th–7th centuries. Senior officers ranged from the commanding *Comes* or *Tribunis*, and *Vicarius* (second in command), to the *Senator, Ducenarius* and *Centenarius*. The old Roman *centurion* rank had become the Byzantine *Ekatontarch*, the most senior

▶ *Here a mounted Christian warrior saint is flanked by two angels on a 6th century Coptic relief carving. He appears to wear scale armour, though this could be a stylized rendition of mail. (Coptic Mus., inv. 6482, Cairo; author's photograph)*

▲ *There is still a lot of argument about where the famous 7th century 'Ashburnham Pentateuch' was made: Egypt, Italy or North Africa. Here Esau carries archery equipment consisting of a quiver* hung on a baldric and a long bowcase of a Central Asian type that would normally only be used by a horseman. (Bib. Nat., Ms. Nouv. Acq. Lat. 2334, Paris)

of whom was second in command to a *Comes* and might also be known as a *Vicarius. Lociservator* was the general term for any deputy officer, while an *Optio* was now a quartermaster. *Auctenta* and *Bandiforus* were ranks normally only found in the east. The *Biarchus, Circitor* and *Semissalis* were junior officers, the *Campiductor* a regimental drill officer, *Draconarii* and *Signiferi* standard-bearers, *Tubatores* trumpeters. *Ilarches* supervised junior officers and the NCOs who led a *Dekarchia* (platoon or section). There were many specialist administrative officers ranging from the *primicerius* (adjutant) to a *Comes* and the *domesticus*, who could be the adjutant of a high official or a member of the *Protectores* (palace guard), to the solely administrative *Pentarchai* and the *Tetrarchai*

responsible for dress and discipline. Surprisingly, given the Byzantine Army's proud Roman heritage, its discipline was now regarded as inferior to that of the Sassanian Persians. Problems with discipline probably lay behind the emphasis given to this subject in military manuals such as the *Strategikon* written by or for the Emperor Maurice.

By the late 6th century, troops were paid annually, probably at the start of winter, and despite irregular payment the men still relied on this during the reign of Heraclius. The army was armed, fed and largely mounted by the state, with each provincial arsenal under a *Sakellarios*. On campaign, local cities were clearly expected to furnish provisions but were often unhappy about doing so. The supply of horses could be an even greater problem, these being the responsibility of the *Comes stabulii*.

The core of the Byzantine Army consisted of the *Comitatus*, basically the Emperor's own force of well-equipped mercenaries. The *Scholae* (palace guard) had become a parade unit, though it remained a source of recruits for high ranking positions, and within the *Scholae* the *Candidati*

OSPREY MILITARY JOURNAL

INTERNATIONAL REVIEW OF MILITARY HISTORY

King Richard III: Villain or Victim?

Mosby snatches a Yankee General

US Marines on the Western Front 1918

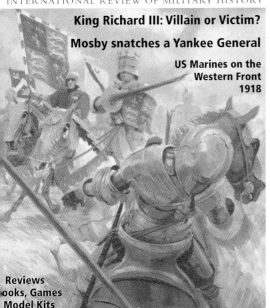

Reviews
ooks, Games
Model Kits

**Fascinating articles on military history
from antiquity to modern times**

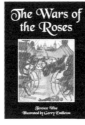

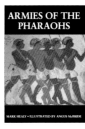

OSPREY MILITARY JOURNAL - From the world's leading publisher of illustrated military history. Bi monthly (six issues per year) 64 pages per issue fully illustrated in Osprey's unique style with artwork, maps, charts and photos. Fascinating articles on military history from ancient times to the present day and expert guidance for enthusiasts.

▶ *Hunting scenes were popular motifs in the mosaics of mid-6th century Byzantine Syria. They illustrate equipment similar to that used in battle, except that the huntsmen wear no armour. Here a man fends off a bear, using a sword and shield. His scabbard hangs from a shoulder baldric, not a belt.(In situ, Church of the Deacon Thomas, 'Ayn Musa, near Mt. Nebo, Jordan.)*

formed an élite, wearing distinctive white uniforms. The *Excubitores* were now the real imperial infantry guard. *Foideratoi* formed the élite of front-line troops, while the *Optimates* formed an élite reserve closer to the capital. Lower in quality and status were the *Bucellarii*, most of whom Maurice had grouped into one large cavalry *Tagma* unit of the field army. Even so, these *Bucellarii* were still better equipped than the bulk of the Byzantine army. The question of whether there were still militarily effective *limitanie* (frontier auxiliary units) in Syria remains unanswered.

Even though the Byzantine Army no longer had real uniforms, it clearly retained a regular unit identification system, each with different shield colours. Flags may have been more important, coming in various sizes, shapes and colours. Byzantine flags were used to control movement, as rallying points and to indicate where a unit should erect its tents. Standard-bearers or *bandiforii* were selected from the bravest and most intelligent men. They wore additional armour for their face and hands, with a second man in support should the *bandiforus* fall. The Byzantine Empire also had many old ceremonial banners and, in contradiction to the teachings of the early Church, icons were also used to instil religious fervour and raise morale.

Under Heraclius the most effective regiments in the east were those in Armenia. The Byzantines were masters of absorbing new military ideas, and Heraclius seems to have been influenced by his Sassanian foes, for example when the élite armoured cavalry were formed into larger units. Nevertheless, the bulk of the Byzantine army still consisted of spear-armed infantry. A new *Praesental* Imperial Army was now mustered in central Anatolia to serve as a mobile force. Considerable debate surrounds the question of when the Byzantine *themes*, or military provinces with their own local armies, first appeared. Something akin to a *theme* was established by Heraclius in 626–8 but was still a regional army rather than a province. Known as the *Opsikion*, it was based in western Anatolia and may have reflected the Sassanian empire's system of separate armies responsible for each frontier.

The Ghassanid Arab *phylarch* or Byzantine frontier ally used his *annona* or payment in gold to keep his people loyal, subsidize allied tribes and

The largely Christian Arab tribes of Syria were richer than those of the Arabian peninsula. They were also militarily much more sophisticated and better equipped. As a result both the Byzantine Empire and the rising power of Islam were eager to win their support. Here a tribal leader is armed and armoured with Byzantine equipment, worn over a tunic and trousers that show Persian influence. The ordinary tribal warrior beside him also has a late Roman helmet, though he wears his hair in long 'Saracen' ringlets. He is dressed in the long izar body-wrap which survives to this day as a Muslim pilgrim's garb. His large infantry bow is of partially composite construction whereas his leather-edged shield is a simple piece of wickerwork. (Angus McBride)

▶ *An archer shoots at a lion, using a composite bow. He holds a second arrow in his left hand. (In situ, Church of the Deacon Thomas, 'Ayn Musa, near Mt. Nebo, Jordan.)*

▶ *A huntsman with a double-ended spear fights an unseen animal. His tunic has decorative claves (patches) indicating that he is a member of the military élite. (In situ, Chapel of Ippolito, Church of the Virgin, Madaba, Jordan; photographs via Studium Biblicum Franciscanum)*

maintain a small guard unit as well as auxiliary troops under local Arab officers. In summer the main Ghassanid leadership lived in settled villages or in small fortified palaces, the most important of which was at Jabiya on the Golan plateau, close to the future battlefield of Yarmuk. These were used as *masani* (military bases) to overawe the nomads, and some seem to have had small barracks. The Golan plateau was, in fact, popular with the Ghassanids, and they had several camping grounds in the area. Other Ghassanid centres were in northern Syria, Jordan and Palestine, mostly well within the frontiers of the Byzantine Empire. For a campaign the Ghassanid tribesmen would leave their flocks in the hands of herdsmen and would place themselves at the disposal of the relevant Byzantine commander.

Byzantine Tactics

Byzantine generalship was in many ways more Greek than Roman, more intellectual and with less emphasis on fierce discipline. Several new military manuals also date from this period, the most famous being the *Strategikon of the Emperor Maurice*. It may, however, have been written early in Heraclius's reign as a practical book for officers before the great war against the Sassanians. The army relied on highly trained, mobile and well equipped forces, a large part consisting of cavalry and mounted infantry armed with spear, sword, bow and shield. Such forces campaigned over great distances. Nevertheless it took several months to move élite forces from the capital to Palestine, while even the moving of local troops risked imposing new burdens of billetting and provisioning on the local inhabitants. After a long move, men and animals needed a long rest, and the Byzantine army, not being a self-sufficient force, depended on exposed supply lines.

In dangerous or uncertain territory a Byzantine army was preceded by light cavalry skirmishers, and at night a field-fortication was erected using supply carts. Byzantine encampments differed from Roman camps in having more and smaller gates for cavalry sorties. According to the *Strategikon*, the wagons surrounding a camp were defended by archers. Behind them was a 10–15 metre wide space, then the tents of the heavy infantry, those of the cavalry and finally a large open space at the centre.

Recent experience against the Sassanians had led the Byzantine army to expect extended campaigns and to avoid big battles, relying on cautious generalship, ambushes and guerrilla tactics. In Syria and Palestine the Byzantines relied on defence in depth supported by small mobile forces to wear down an enemy. The civilian population was expected to take refuge within walled towns. In fact, raids rather than invasions were expected, and these could be dealt with by local garrisons, while long-range patrolling was left to Arab auxiliaries such as the Ghassanids.

In battle, archery with the recently introduced heavier Avar bow was the most important offensive tactic. Archery training emphasized power and accuracy rather than the speed of shooting, this being considered a matter of practice. Men were also trained to use three different archery draws to avoid fatigue.

Infantry and cavalry were trained to change front, turn and wheel, the failure of one such tactic perhaps precipitating the Byzantine defeat at Yarmuk. Traditionally, Byzantine cavalry drew up in

▼ *Archetypal army formations: A: Late 6th to early 7th century Byzantine cavalry; B: Late 6th to early 7th century Byzantine infantry (based on the 'Strategikon' attributed to the Emperor Maurice);*

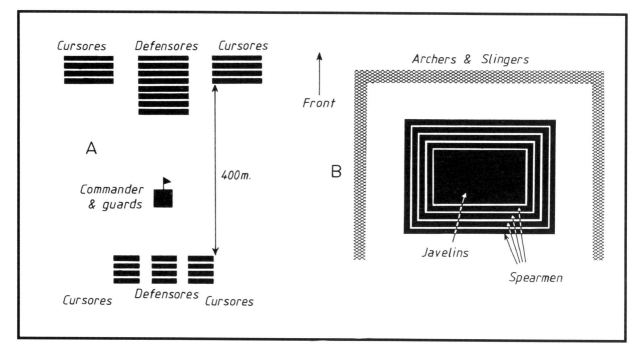

A

Cursores Defensores Cursores

Commander & guards

400m.

Front

Cursores Defensores Cursores

B

Archers & Slingers

Javelins

Spearmen

three extended divisions, but new formations in the *Strategikon* were designed to be more manoeuverable. Two types of troops were involved: the *Cursores*, who advanced in open order to attack with bows and then retreat if counter-charged; and *Defensores*, who protected these archers. The flanks largely consisted of *Cursores*, the centre of *Defensores*. The other role of Byzantine heavy cavalry was to pin down the front of an enemy formation while light cavalry worked around their flanks and rear.

Armour for cavalrymen and horses was mostly for protection against archery, and *Cataphracti* remained the cavalry élite. But the most typical late 6th century Byzantine horseman was a 'composite' lance-bow trooper equipped in an essentially Persian-Turkish manner. Horse-archery was, of course, more accurate when the animal was standing still, but whatever the circumstances a horse-archer was always vulnerable if attacked from the right by a lancer. Hence formations constantly tried to outflank each other while defending their own right with reinforcements. Much has been made of the disadvantages suffered by cavalrymen before the introduction of stirrups, particularly those armed with spears. It was, however, clearly possible to use these weapons effectively without stirrups if the rider had some kind of supporting saddle, and a two-handed manner of wielding the spear had been used in the Middle East since post-Hellenistic times.

The main infantry strength of Byzantine armies lay in their bowmen. Infantry archers had been the main strength of Syrian armies throughout the Roman period, their primary role being to disrupt enemy cavalry and hamper their ability to deliver a charge. According to Byzantine military manuals the first two ranks of infantry archers shot at the horses' legs, the rear ranks aiming high to drop their arrows on the enemy, who could not use their shields to protect themselves and their animals at the same time. This long-established Middle Eastern tradition of infantry archery would decline in the face of Central Asian archery traditions from the late 7th century onwards, but it was still important during the Yarmuk campaign. In the *Strategikon* foot soldiers consisted of heavy *Skoutatoi* and light *Psiloi*, normally drawn up in rectangular formations. The front rank would have shields one and half metres wide so that they could overlap and form a 'shield wall'. Byzantine light infantry, with slings, bows or javelins, operated as skirmishers to harrass enemy cavalry or operate on the flanks.

Byzantium was regarded as particularly strong in siege warfare. Frontiers and rear areas were covered by walled cities, with many smaller *castella* providing defence in depth, while in Syria there had been a noticeable militarization of the local administration. A little known mid-6th century Byzantine military treatise, probably written by an army engineer, described the role of frontier forts as observation points and places where troops could assemble before a raid. If attacked, a garrison would drop powdered lime, boiling water or hot ashes on the enemy. Melted (not 'boiling') pitch, with or without sulphur, could be poured on an enemy's wooden siege engines and then set ablaze. The walls of a fort could be protected with padded mats pegged to the top of the walls or by netting hung one metre outside the wall. Artillery on walls and towers also defended the gates.

The use of terror in warfare was more highly developed in 'civilized' Byzantium than among its less advanced neighbours. While military manuals like the *Strategikon* laid down rules to stop troops doing unnecessary damage, it was common for the heads and hands of defeated enemies to be paraded in public. On other occasions captives were publicly tortured and then executed in full view of an enemy in order to inspire fear.

Byzantine Weaponry

Byzantium was always short of iron, and in the 6th century the manufacture of weaponry, or at least of armour, had been made a state monopoly in *Armamenton* (arsenals) established in cities such as Alexandria, Antioch and Damascus. Swords may have been made more widely, and hunting weapons like bows would have been readily available, the provinces of Syria, Palestine and Arabia perhaps being the main areas of bow making throughout the Roman and Byzantine periods. In fact, Byzantium's shortage of arms meant that enemy weaponry was always carefully collected – Sassanian equipment

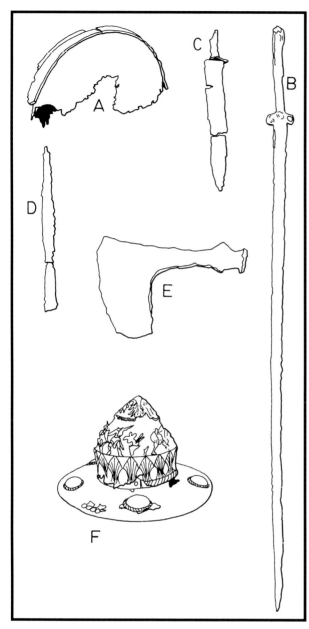

◀ *Byzantine weaponry.*
A: Two-piece iron helmet
from Hadithah on the
Dead Sea, 4th–7th
centuries. (Castle
Museum, Karak,
Jordan); B: Cavalry
sword, almost two metres
long and probably
symbolic, from
Aphrodisias, 6th–7th
centuries. (Archaeological
Museum, Aphrodisias,
Turkey); C: Iron dagger
with bronze guard from
Hadithah, 4th–7th
centuries. (Castle
Museum, Karak,
Jordan); D: Iron
spearhead from Corinth,
6th–7th centuries.
(Archaeological Museum,
Athens, Greece); E: Iron
axe-blade from Butrint,
6th–8th centuries.
(Museum of Archaeology,
Tirana, Albania); F:
Gilded bronze shield-boss
from Nocera Umbra, 7th
century. (Museo dell'Alto
Medio Evo, Rome, Italy).

century AD, and a century later Turkish Avar influence was clearly apparent in Byzantine cavalry dress. The decoration of buckles and other small items confirm this strong Avar influence. An officer's distinctive *scaramangion* (coat) was the same as the Persian horseman's *kaftan*. *Candidati* (guardsmen) also received a *maniakion* (cape or cloak) with three buttons on the chest. This was a mark of the élite and could be worn with a highly decorated belt. Byzantine infantry costume now seems to have reflected Germanic Goth influence.

The *Strategikon* provides a lot of information about early 7th century Byzantine weaponry. The cavalry were armed with a long *spathion* (sword) of Avar or Sassanian origin. They would also have a light wooden *kontarion* (lance) and a *toxarion* (bow) with 40 arrows in a quiver hung from the saddle or from a belt. A bowcase may have been attached to the saddle in Persian style or hung from the belt in the Central Asian nomad manner. Heavy infantry *Skoutatoi* had the shorter *Spathion Erouliskion* in addition to a short spear or javelin. Byzantine light troops carried a small shield, a bow across the back, *thekarion* (quiver) with flap hung from the shoulder rather than a belt, and possibly a *solenarion* ('arrow-guide') to shoot short darts. Or they could be armed with heavy and light *akontion* and *berutta* (javelins) or with a sling.

The *Strategikon* also lists armour, that of the cavalry ideally consisting of a long *zaba* or *lorikion* (mail hauberk) with a *skaplion* (mail coif) and a helmet with a pendant *peritrachelion* (throat defence) lined with fabric and having a fringe. The

was particularly prized. The possession of weapons was itself strictly regulated. The Byzantine soldier received his first issue of kit on enlistment. He was then expected to buy replacements from his yearly allowance: one third on clothing, one third on weaponry and one third on other needs. Anything lost in battle would be replaced by the state – but not if it had been thrown away in flight.

Although only the élite guard units wore real uniforms, soldiers did have distinctive dress. The influence of 'enemy' Persian fashions had been seen among the Greek élite of Syria since the 3rd

▶ *During the 6th century the Romano-Byzantine army was strongly influenced by hostile neighbouring peoples; Central Asian and Avar styles being adopted by the cavalry, continuing Germanic influence being seen in infantry equipment. This was particularly obvious in the use of lameller armour for rider and horse, as seen on Thracian Byzantine cavalry; whereas the Byzantine guards infantryman shown here only has a short mail shirt. (Angus McBride)*

chassis (helmet) seems to have been heavy, plumed and possibly with cheek-pieces. Some Byzantine cavalrymen also wore *straggulion* (wool-lined gorgets) copied from their Avar foes, but only élite *Bucellarii* had *cheiromanika* (arm guards). The best *Skoutatoi* infantry similarly had mail hauberks and helmets, those in more exposed positions also wearing *periknemides* (leg-defences). But most Byzantine infantry were not weighed down with armour, only having light helmets of Sassanian form and carrying large shields.

A little known source of *c.*615 described one *lorikion* as a 'triple layered *zaba*' weighing 25 kilos. Lighter lamellar or scale armour was used, though not as much as in following centuries. Padded leather, felt or quilted armour was used where better protection was unavailable, the *lorikion alusidoton* being a leather cuirass perhaps of scale or lamellar construction. The *kentouklon* was a form of perhaps quilted 'soft armour' for men and horses, while the *kabadion* seems to have been a quilted armour often used ceremonially. Another distinctive piece of Byzantine equipment was the *kamelaukion* (padded or quilted hood) worn over a helmet and made in the same way as the padded *epilorikon*.

By the 4th century the 'four-horned saddle', normally associated with Roman cavalry, had been replaced by a more modern looking saddle with raised pommel and cantle. As stirrups had not yet been adopted, this would seem to have provided the rider with less stability! Unless stirrups were known (but neither illustrated nor mentioned for a further three centuries) the mystery remains unsolved. Scholars have concentrated on the degree of stability that the Roman 'horned saddle' gave to a cavalryman wielding a spear or sword, but this saddle was never used in Central Asia when the main weapon was the bow. One may therefore assume that it was unsuited to horse archery, which was in fact increasingly important in Middle Eastern warfare. So perhaps there was an unrecognized connection between the rise of Byzantine, Syrian and perhaps Sassanian horse archery and this abandonment of the 'horned saddle'. *Skalia* (stirrups) are, however, mentioned in the *Strategikon*, though only being used by medical personnel to help wounded men. Again, scholars have probably over-emphasized the importance of stirrups in cavalry warfare, the most immediate effect of using them being to reduce fatigue when riding long distances.

The Size of Byzantine Armies

Although the Byzantine army was much larger than that of the Muslim Arab invaders, the sizes of the forces Heraclius could put into the field were smaller than those of a century earlier. On the eve of the Muslim invasion there were probably 10–20,000 élite troops around the capital Constantinople, 25,000 second rate troops in Egypt, a further 5–10,000 in Africa, 5–10,000 in Byzantine Italy, 8–10,000 in the Balkans, 5,000 on the Mediterranean islands, 12,000 tied down in Armenia (of whom only 5–8,000 were available for duty elsewhere), 1–2,000 in Isauria and Cilicia, 8,000 in Upper Mespotamia, 5,000 in northern Syria, plus 5,000 in Palestine and Arabia. A further 6,000 tribesmen from allied Arab *phylarchs* could be added to this total.

At most, 50,000 non-Arab troops could be used against the Muslims, but half of these were tied down in garrisons or defending communications. Many of the remainder were unavailable because the Empire could not pay them. In fact 6–7th century Byzantine expeditionary forces never exceeded 20–30,000 troops – cavalry and infantry. The larger garrisons ranged from around 1,500 at Antioch to several hundred at Chalcis (Qinnasrin) and 200–300 mobile troops at Caesarea Maritima (Qaysariya). Most other garrisons consisted of one or two hundred men, often assimilated into the local population.

Muslim Recruitment

The first Muslim conquests were carried out by selected warriors, not by mass tribal migrations. Nevertheless, the entire male Muslim community had theoretical military obligations; the term *jaysh* referring to something like a 'people's army'. *'Asabiya* or tribal loyalty was very strong and contributed to the remarkable morale of Muslim Arab troops during the early campaigns. However, the Arabian tribes had very limited manpower resources, with only their greater mobility and fighting ability to compensate for their lack of numbers.

Most fighting men in Arabian towns and oases fought as infantry in an essentially defensive manner, and with the coming of Islam they enjoyed a higher military status than the unreliable nomadic bedouin cavalry whose conversion was often only skin-deep. Very little is known about Arab horsemen during this early period. The pre-Islamic Arab Lakhmid rulers on the frontiers of Iraq seem to have relied on Sassanian Persian *asawira* (professional cavalry) rather than tribal troopers, and the Sassanians also sent *asawira* to bolster Arab allies in Yamama (north-eastern Saudi Arabia), Oman and Yemen. A force of 800 *asawira* fought its way to Yemen in the mid-6th century and the descendants of a Sassanian occupation force were still there when the Prophet Muhammad's troops conquered the country. Now known as *abna'*, they

◀ ▶ *Left and right: Camels and huntsmen appear on this 6th–7th century relief carving of 'The Labours of the Months' from Egypt. The camel was the main beast of burden for early Muslim Arab armies. The huntsman on the right carries a large recurved, perhaps composite bow, seemingly with its bowstring unstrung. (Coptic Mus., inv. 7962 & 7964, Cairo; author's photograph)*

fought hard for Islam during the Riddah Wars and probably during the great Muslim Arab conquests that followed.

The indigenous armies of southern Arabia were organized in a different manner from those of the north. There was a fully developed state apparatus with kings and an *ashraf* (nobility) including *qails* or (tribal 'dukes') responsible for law and order. In this they were supported by hereditary classes of administrators and warriors. The Yemeni military system soon provided large numbers of infantry, including camel-riding mounted infantry, to the Muslim armies. In fact, Yemeni troops played a significant role in the conquest of Byzantine Syria.

Nor did these first armies only include Muslims. Christian Arabs fought for Islam against the Sassanians in Iraq, while the first Muslim invaders of Byzantine territory may have been helped by Jewish Arab tribes in what is now southern Jordan. Non-Arabs also played a part. At one time the *Ahabish* (paid warriors) of Makka were thought to have been Abyssinian slaves; they are now known to have been drawn from a confederation of small tribes including men of African origin. One tradition states that 'Amr Ibn al Amr had black soldiers with him when he invaded Egypt a few decades later. There were also many Semitic but non-Arab peoples near the coasts of what are now Oman, Hadramawt, Dhufar and Yemen. Some still live in Dhufar.

Muslim Military Organization

The word *jihad*, despite the way it is used by modern journalists, never simply meant 'Holy War'. It was, and still is, the struggle to strengthen Islam both within an individual's soul and in the world at large. The great 'Umar, second Caliph of Islam, is credited with formalizing rules of behaviour for his soldiers, and though they clearly have their roots in the Quran these instructions are remarkably similar to those in Byzantine military manuals such as the *Strategikon*.

Operations were carefully planned and coordinated. Volunteers were summoned from specified tribes, but they then served in organized armies, not tribal hordes. Troops mustered at specified points usually near Madina, the first capital of the new Islamic state, before the armies were sent where the Caliph decided. There is, however, little information about the *muqatila* ('fighters') themselves during this early period. Some families went with the army to look after flocks for food, tend the wounded and maintain morale, but there were never many of them. The tribal structure was the basis of military organization, the men being paid through their tribe, and when 'Umar visited Syria the troops were ordered to present themselves by *'Ashira* or clan. There was also a parallel non-tribal organization within the army based upon military functions such as cavalry or infantry.

Less is known about the early Islamic command structure than that of the Byzantine army, and it was probably much less elaborate. *Walis* (provincial governors) were, however, responsible for preparing and organizing regional armies, estimating their costs and sending them against the enemy. These *walis* divided any booty gained, retaining one fifth for their own administrative costs. The structure of armies may have reflected Byzantine practice. An *amir* (commanding officer) appointed divisional or field commanders known as *umara al tabiya* under whom were the *umara al ashar* ('commanders of tens'). Other officer ranks included *ashab al rayat* ('standard bearers'), *quwwad* ('leaders') and the *ru'us al qaba'il* ('tribal chiefs').

The chain of command is unclear but may have gone from the *amir* to field commanders,

▲ *The clearest illustration of an early Muslim Arab warrior wearing a headcloth is on this damaged fragment of wall-painting from early 8th century Penjikent in what is now Uzbekistan.*

It is looped beneath his chin, a style that continued to be used by bedouin and in North Africa throughout the Middle Ages. (Oriental Dept., State Hermitage Mus., St. Petersburg)

commanders of ten, standard bearers, *quwwad* officers and finally tribal chiefs. This would suggest that tribal identification was seen only at a very low level. Seniority was based upon proven loyalty to Islam, and on one occasion 'Umar told a commander not to allow the leaders of former Riddah rebels to command more than 100 men, though he was allowed to consult them on purely military matters. The tribe was subdivided into *'irafa* (pay units) which may also have served as squads in battle.

More is known about the *Khayl* (cavalry) than the infantry. The *faris* (horseman) probably had more in common with his Sassanian than Byzantine counterpart, and he formed part of a tribally based *qatiba* or (squadron). The *kurdus* was a smaller sub-unit of cavalry. Other cavalry terms included the *mujarrada* (battle formation), *tali'a* and *sari'a* (reconnaissance or raid), *jarida* (independent long-range raiding force), and *rabita* (mobile garrison based in a conquered town).

Of the various kinds of banner the *liwa'* came to represent military command, the *raya* being a mark of kinship or a personal flag. Standard bearers were drawn from reliable tribal leaders and sometimes wore turbans of the same colour as their tribal banner. Each tribe had its own banner in pre-Islamic times, and, although the early Caliphs mistrusted the use of flags other than those of the Prophet Muhammad himself, Abu Bakr did order commanders in Syria to assign special banners to each unit: for example, the élite non-tribal *Muhajirun* marched behind a yellow flag with white, green and black markings. It is also worth noting that the Crescent was as yet a non-Muslim insignia associated with the pagan moon gods of southern Arabia and with the Sassanians.

The *'ata* (pay-system) was only in an embryonic form during the conquest of Syria. In addition, a soldier would receive his share of the *fay* or booty, a cavalryman getting three times as much as a foot soldier because his expenses were higher.

Tactics of the Muslim Forces

The tactics used by early Muslim armies reflected the influence of the Byzantine and Sassanian empires, modified by the Arabs' lack of horses but possession of camels. Sassanian infantry archers normally advanced in ordered ranks shooting volleys of arrows on command, followed by a charge. It was probably the same in Arab armies. Sassanian archers were renowned for the speed with which they shot, rather than for the power of their bows, whereas the Arabs were like the Byzantines in shooting more slowly with heavier arrows.

Early Muslim Arab armies were smaller and more mobile than those of their foes. Largely self-sufficient, they did not rely on long supply routes, nor were they deterred from operating deep inside enemy territory. The Arabs' famous ability to withdraw into the desert depended on their superior knowledge of grazing and water sources. Mounted infantry rode camels, while the cavalry also led their war-horses from camelback until the moment of battle. The Arabs' superior mobility was strategic rather than tactical, and cavalry could be held up by natural obstacles such as the *Harra* (lava plains), mountains, marshes, rivers, irrigation

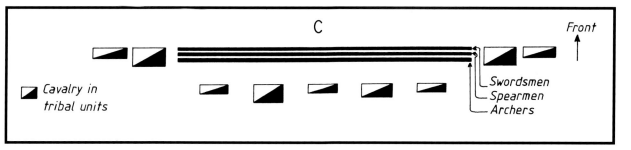

C

Front

Cavalry in
tribal units

Swordsmen
Spearmen
Archers

▲ *Mid-7th century Arab-Islamic army (after A. von Pawlikowski-Cholewa)*

ditches and sandy desert. Even with the wood-framed north Arabian saddle, camels could not make proper cavalry charges and were notoriously unresponsive to their riders' commands. Camels did, however, carry provisions, mules being found more suitable in the mountains.

Traditional Arab warfare consisted of raids designed to weaken an enemy's ability to survive in a harsh climate. Casualties were small, with a code of military conduct intended to minimize unnecessary losses. Such warfare led to an intellectual approach that admired crafty stratagems and also accepted that withdrawing before a superior force was honourable. Islam expanded upon this military heritage and the *siyar* ('rules of war') were based upon a typical condemnation of all forms of excess. The Muslims also introduced a new obedience to orders and a willingness to accept higher casualties.

Almost all battles were associated with roads, a factor unnoticed by scholars, who have assumed that the highly mobile Arabs were uninterested in traditional arteries of communication. In most cases the Muslim Arab armies fought defensively,

anchoring their infantry positions on natural obstacles like hills or lava plains while the small Muslim cavalry forces were reserved for outflanking movements. Their emphasis on defensive infantry tactics naturally affected the battle-array used, which tended to be simple. Men were drawn up in *Sufuf* (ranks) and would also advance in line of battle. Whether or not the fully developed *Khamis* ('five division') plan was used before the Umayyad period is unclear, but it seems to appear at Yarmuk. The same was true of the *tabi'a* ('close formations'). The five divisions of *Khamis* were the *muqaddama* (advance guard), *qalb* (centre), *maimanah* (right wing), *maisarah* (left wing) and *saqah* (rearguard).

A century or so later, Arab divisional units were described as being a bowshot apart, companies taking turns to fight so as to conserve energy. Against the Sassanians in Iraq, the Muslim Arab infantry were, on at least one occasion, placed at the centre with mixed cavalry and infantry divisions on

▶ *This relief carving of 'Daniel in the Lions' Den' comes from Alcaudete in southern Spain and is generally thought to date from the late 5th or 6th century. The Babylonian warriors, however, wear decorated headcloths that could indicate they are based on the first Muslim Arab invaders of Spain in the early 8th century, as such costume is otherwise unknown in the area. (Museo Arqueológico, Madrid)*

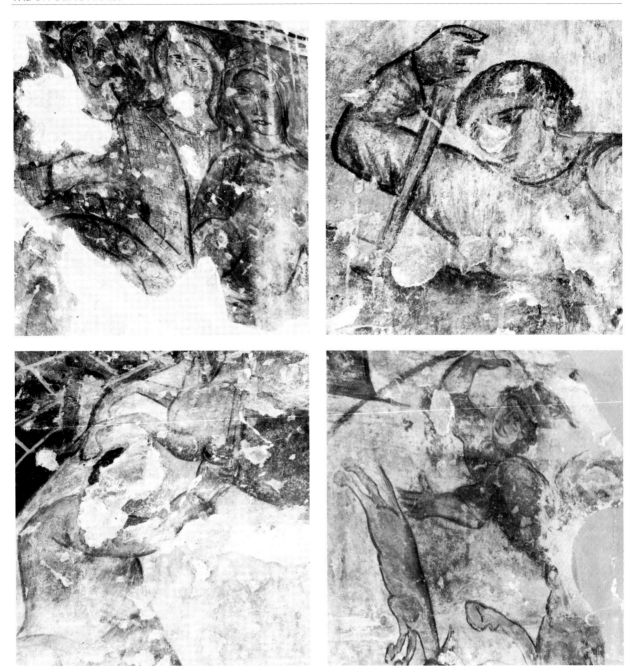

the flanks. A unique document from 647 states that Muslim infantry were more heavily armoured than the cavalry, and various accounts of early Muslim heroes show that the most common wounds were to the lower legs and feet, the least common to shoulders, hands or torso. Many lost eyes to arrows, while others died from arrows in the throat. Such evidence suggests infantry combat using swords and large shields, with archery as an important secondary threat.

The Arabs had long been known for their use of noise to intimidate a foe. The normal Muslim battle-cry of *Allahu Akbar* ('God is most Powerful') could be repeated as a signal for prearranged action – for example, firstly for men to don their armour, secondly for units to get in position, thirdly to send forward the *mubarizun* (champions) and lastly to indicate a general advance. Duels between champions had been a feature of pre-Islamic Arab, Byzantine and Sassanian warfare for a long time.

◀ *The famous early Islamic wall-paintings in the reception hall at Qusayr 'Amra portray weapons and military costume very clearly. Guardsmen (far left), one of whom rests his arms on a large round shield. All wear headcloths similar to those on the supposedly pre-Islamic relief carving from Alcaudete. Another painted wall shows the slaughter of animals for food at the end of a desert hunt. One man (near left) stabs with a short sword; another (bottom left) strikes with a similar weapon using both hands. At one end of a desert hunting scene a rider (bottom right) falls from*

his horse. Elsewhere the horsemen clearly ride without stirrups. Was the artist commenting on the Arabs' well-documented unwillingness to adopt new-fangled stirrups? (in situ, Qusayr 'Amra, Jordan; author's photographs)

▶ *A series of primitive painted figures on the ceiling at Qusayr 'Amra include this horseman. He clearly rides without stirrups and wears a large headcloth, apparently beneath his chin, billowing out behind him. (in situ, Qusayr 'Amra, Jordan, author's photograph)*

Mubarizun were also a recognized part of a Muslim army, their role being to undermine an enemy's morale by slaying his champions. Infantry would then make repeated charges and withdrawals known as *karr wa farr*, using spears and swords, similar to the Byzantine cavalry tactics of *Cursores* and *Defensores*. Nevertheless, the Muslims still tended to reserve their main effort for a counter-attack after the enemy had worn himself out.

Pre-Islamic Arabs are said to have used archery more for hunting than for war, but the widespread denigration of early Arab archery springs from a misunderstanding of the 7th century evidence. Whereas the Central Asian Turks were horse archers, Arab archers were infantry who proved themselves very effective against enemy cavalry. The Sassanians, for example, mocked the Arabs for their slow rate of fire but then found that the despised 'spindle-like' Muslim arrows easily penetrated armour. One detailed account of such an archer described him emptying his quiver on the ground, kneeling and preparing to shoot. The maximum useful range of a traditional Arab bow was around 150 metres.

Arab cavalry *foederati* in Byzantine service were described as attacking in wedge-shaped Romano-Byzantine *cuneos* formations. Subsequent Muslim Arab cavalry operated on the wings or through the centre, making flanking or encircling movements after their infantry had disrupted the enemy, their main task being to destroy an already defeated foe. These traditions later came in for considerable criticism, as reported by the early 9th century Iraqi scholar al Jahiz. Here the non-Arab critic said:

'Your spears were of *murran* wood [a particularly flexible material] and your spear-points of cow-horn. In war you rode your horses bareback and if you had a saddle it was like a (frameless padded) leather camel-saddle. You do not have stirrups though stirrups improve the thrust with a spear and the blow with a sword for you can rise up in them or lean against them.... You also boast of the length of your *Rumh* spear and the shortness of the sword, yet it is vainglorious for the infantryman to boast of the shortness of his sword while he is inferior to the horseman.... But the strength of the horseman rests in the strength of his hand and the length and breadth of his sword.'

The Arab in al Jahiz' work then retorted:

'As far as the history of stirrups is concerned, all [the evidence] indicates that these are ancient.... Although the Arabs did not use it, they knew of it.... However they preferred to mount their horses by leaping on to them. 'Umar Ibn al Khattab (the second Caliph, ruling at the time of the battle of

Yarmuk) said, "He who constantly leaps and dismounts will not grow weak".... According to 'Umar when the *Muhajirun* and the *Ansar* (two of the first groups of Muslims during Muhammad's own lifetime) increased in number they included many whose habits were foreign, but they removed their stirrups and started mounting their horses by leaping on them.'

The Arab spokesman saw no reason to comment on the famous short swords of the early Muslim Arabs.

In camp the Muslim Arabs left their camels with servants. The only other information about Arab encampments concerns their tents and the heavy tent-poles, which could be used as weapons in an emergency. Early Muslim Arab armies are also popularly believed to have been incapable of siege warfare, but this is again a misunderstanding. Settled Arab tribes clearly had some siege capabilities. Several of the tallest houses in the Ghassanid town of Umm al Jimal were intended to be defensible and still have machicolations from

◀ *Late Sassanian* **Asvaran** *cavalry and a* **Berber** *tribesman. A number of Sassanian Persian troops were left in Syria after the Byzantine reconquest and they then fought for the Byzantines at Yarmouk. Many others would soon be recruited into Muslim ranks in Iraq and Iran. In addition to his low-domed iron helmet this horseman is protected by a lamellar bard covering only the front of its body, neck and head. This horseman's use of wooden stirrups raises the unsolved question of when and where the Persians first adopted stirrups. Berber troops supported Heraclius in his original struggle for the Byzantine throne. This warrior is, however, equipped in the simplest style used by ordinary Berber tribesmen.(Angus McBride)*

which missiles could be dropped. Written sources mention similar tribal houses in Madina, defended by archers and rock-throwers on the roof. Some of these oasis houses even had their own stone-throwing engines and rams to attack rival houses. Ta'if, supposedly the 'only fortified town in Arabia', had a wall of brick or stone bonded with mud and surrounded by a deep ditch. To the south, Yemen had been a land of castles and fortified towns for centuries, while Oman also had several large fortifications. Most of the early Muslim conquests were, in fact, achieved by siege warfare rather than by large-scale battles. Prolonged blockades, luring a garrison out into the open to be destroyed, capturing enemy leaders for ransom, or harrying the agricultural surroundings to force a town to make

▲ *Some Coptic ivory carvings made after the Muslim conquest of Egypt, like this* **situla** *probably dating from the 7th or 8th century, do show horsemen using stirrups. The short sword and extremely simple form of bridle may indicate Arab influence. (Walters Art Gall., Baltimore)*

terms, were the generally preferred tactics. Even so, the Muslims used a stone-throwing *manjaniq* (mangonel) against the walls of Damascus as early as 635.

Weaponry of the Muslim Forces

The dress of early Muslim warriors would have reflected their immediate cultural background.

Whereas the Arab nomad wore a long *izar* cloth wrapped several times around his body, urban Arabs and those living closer to the Byzantine and Sassanian frontiers would often have dressed in the same tunics and cloaks as their neighbours. *Sirwal* (trousers) would soon become the mark of a soldier and were of Persian origin, while the Yemeni élite wore silks and cosmetics – to the disgust of more pious Muslims.

During the Middle Ages it was almost obligatory for a Muslim Arab to shave his head, but in pre-Islamic times the Arabs wore long hair, and this still seems to have been the case among many early Muslims. Even a senior military leader could still wear his hair in four stiff plaits. It was the loose *'imama* (head-cloth) that distinguished the northern and central Arabs, but this was not yet a true turban in the later medieval or modern sense. It was probably normal to wear some form of cap beneath an *'imama* – Khalid Ibn al Walid was to lose just such a favourite red cap during the battle of Yarmuk. Heavy leather sandals were also typical of the early Muslim Arabs, Roman type sandal-boots also having been found in the graves of pre-Islamic Arab auxiliary troops in Jordan.

The weaponry of the early Muslims is likely to have been as mixed as their costume. During the immediate pre-Islamic period most Arabian military equipment seems to have come from Syria, Iraq, Armenia and Yemen; a great deal more would then have been captured during the early conquests. Much armour made in Iraq, along the Gulf coast, in Oman and Yemen was of hardened leather scale or lamellar construction rather than of iron. The largely Christian town of Najran in northern Yemen was already an important centre of arms manufacture during Muhammad's lifetime, but again it was famous for leather rather than for iron. The peace agreement that Najran made with its Muslim conquerors stipulated that the town supply 30 sets of armour, 30 horses and 30 camels for operations along the Gulf coast or in Yemen. The Caliph 'Umar soon transported the Christians of Najran to southern Iraq. This was already a largely Christian area and, rather than being intended to remove a potentially subversive non-Islamic population, it was more likely to have reflected the Najranis' role as skilled armourers at a time when

▶ *Muslim weaponry. A: Late Sassanian-early Islamic segmented helmet from Nineveh, 5th–7th centuries. (British Museum. London, England); B: Late Sassanian-early Islamic segmented helmet from Nineveh, 7th century. (British Museum. London, England); C: One-piece iron helmet from Varaghsah, Transoxania, early 8th century. (Museum of Uzbek History, Samarqand, Uzbekistan); D: One-piece reed 'Bow of the Prophet Muhammad', traditionally mid-7th century. (Islamic Reliquary, Topkapi Palace Museum, Istanbul, Turkey); E: 'Sword of the Caliph 'Uthman' with later hilt, traditionally mid-7th century. (Islamic Reliquary, Topkapi Palace Museum, Istanbul, Turkey); F:* 'Sword of the Caliph 'Umar' with later hilt, traditionally mid-7th century. (Islamic Reliquary, Topkapi Palace Museum, Istanbul, Turkey); G: Late Sassanian or early Islamic sword from Oman, 5th–7th centuries. (location unknown); H: 'Sword of Khalid Ibn al Walid' with later hilt, traditionally mid-7th century. (Islamic Reliquary, Topkapi Palace Museum, Istanbul, Turkey); I: Iron dagger with bronze guard from Pella, early-mid-8th century (location unknown); J: iron sword-guard from al Rabadhah, 7th–9th centuries. (Dept. of Archaeology, King Sa'ud University, Saudi Arabia); K: iron knife with wooden grip from Qasr Ibrim, Nubia, 8th–9 centuries. (British Museum. London, England)

southern Iraq was the base for operations in Iran.

Although Najran was famous for its leather, the swords of Yemen appear to have been made from imported ingots of high quality Indian *wootz*, an early form of steel. Other, inferior, blades were made elsewhere in Arabia and along the borders of Syria. Long-shafted spears were made locally from the reeds of the Gulf coast. Bows were also made in various parts of Arabia, the most typical being the Hijazi bow. It could be of one piece of wood, or two strips joined back to back, and it was up to two metres long when unbraced – roughly the same size as the famous English longbow.

The nomads always depended on settled people for metal goods, and the many annual tribal fairs held around Arabia served as distribution centres. Another tradition suggests that powerful Jewish Arab tribes in northern Hijaz served as a channel for weaponry from the pro-Byzantine Ghassanids

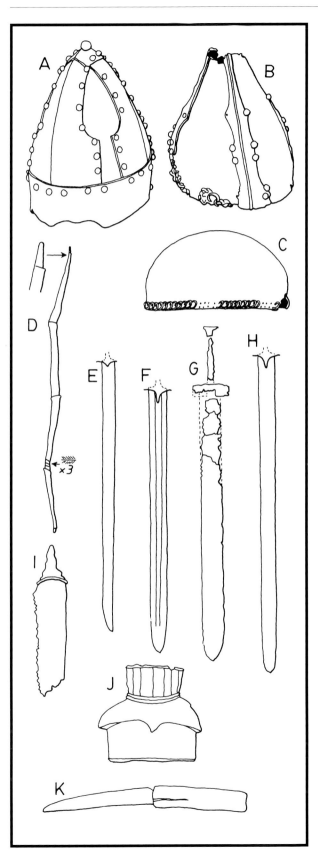

and the pro-Sassanian Lakhmids to their various allies within Arabia. On defeating these Jewish tribes the first Muslims captured a substantial supply of arms and armour, the Banu Nadhir supplying 50 sets of armour, 50 helmets, 340 swords, and the Banu Quraiza no fewer than 1,500 swords, 300 sets of armour, 1,000 spears, 1,500 shields and perhaps even stone-throwing machines from their tribal castles.

In fact, the early Muslim armies probably had adequate equipment when the conquests began, though less than their Byzantine and Sassanian foes. Several *Hadiths* or 'Sayings of the Prophet and Companions' dealt with the problems of military supply. For example: 'When a man is given something to use on a military expedition and he brings it to the battlefield, then it remains his; or if a man promises to go on campaign but is prevented by his parents he should accept their decision but go next year; as for the equipment, he should store it until he needs it; if he fears it will be spoiled let him sell it and keep the money so that he can buy what he needs for another expedition.'

The armour itself included gilded helmets, perhaps similar to the silvered helmets found in the Sassanian Empire. One surviving helmet from the late Sassanian or early Islamic period has the remains of a mail *aventail*, while another seems to have the fragments of a leather lining. Early Arab written sources refer to both pointed and rounded helmets. The former were probably of segmented construction like those seen in Turkish central Asia and may have been called *tarikah*. The *baidah* ('egg') helmet was more common and may have been similar to the standard two-piece early Byzantine type. Mail was commonly used to protect the face, cheeks and neck, either as an *aventail* from the helmet or as a *mighfar* (mail coif) such as had been seen in Romano-Byzantine armies since the 5th century.

The normal body armour was the *dir'*, a large mail hauberk, which opened part-way down the chest. A *dir'* would be polished and stored in a mixture of dust, oil and camel dung to stop rusting. A remarkable document of 647 mentions a force of 342 soldiers being accompanied by twelve 'mail makers'. Lamellar armour had been rare even in Sassanian Iran, and the few *jawshan* cuirasses used

Composite cavalry, equipped as both horse-archers and close-combat spearmen, were the shock troops of the early 7th century Byzantine Empire. Many Byzantine soldiers also seem to have adopted the Persian fashion of wearing a decorative cap over their helmet. The unarmoured military commander shown here illustrates the mixture of magnificence and barbarity characteristic of the Christian early Byzantine Empire. His style of costume eventually evolved into medieval church vestments. Around his neck is a heavy gold necklace marking his rank. But he also raises aloft the severed hand and head of a defeated rebel – another Byzantine practice.(Angus McBride)

by Sassanians and some of their Muslim Arab conquerors were very expensive.

A conversation attributed to the Caliph 'Umar and 'Amr Ibn al As summed up the early Islamic warrior's opinions on the merits of various weapons. 'The javelin?' asked Amr. 'It is a brother which might betray you.' 'The arrows?' 'Arrows are messengers of death which might miss or might hit.' 'The shield?' 'That is the protection which suffers most.' 'The coat of mail?' 'Something which keeps the horseman busy, is a nuisance to the foot soldier but is in all cases a strong protection.' 'The sword?' 'It might be the cause of *your* death!'

Most shields were clearly of leather, mostly camel- or cow-hide, and would be kept supple with oil as had been done in the Middle East since the days of the ancient Hebrews. Infantry spears were about two and a half metres long, those of the cavalry up to five and a half metres. A wife's veil could be tied on as a pennon, a typically romantic Arab idea that later spread to medieval Europe. Javelins were used, particularly by Yemeni troops.

The sword was by far the most prestigious Arab weapon and was a short infantry weapon like the Roman *gladius*. Some Arab warriors carried two swords, though this might have referred to horsemen with both short Arab swords and longer Sassanian cavalry blades. Meanwhile the dagger, in Arabia as in Iran, was a personal weapon and the last line of defence.

The Size of Muslim Forces

The total Muslim number of fighting men during the Caliphate of 'Umar may have reached 50,000, but the size of the armies that invaded the huge neighbouring empires was often tiny. The first armies sent into Byzantine territory soon proved to be too small, although there were several separate Muslim forces operating in Syria and Palestine. Those of Shurahbil, Yazid and subsequently Abu 'Ubaida each had around 7,000 men and 'Amr only 3,000. This total included cavalry forces, some 3,300 Quraysh, 1,700 from the bedouin Sulaim tribe and around 700 of the Murad tribe from Yemen. After Khalid Ibn al Walid led his reinforcements across the desert from Iraq, the Muslims were able to concentrate 15–18,000 men at the battle of Ajnadayn, where they defeated 9–10,000 Byzantines. Estimates of the size of the Muslim Arab army at Yarmuk vary from 20,000 to 40,000, but it was probably more like 25,000 – and this time they were greatly outnumbered by the Byzantines.

▶ *Arabs appear in several Coptic carvings from Byzantine and early Islamic Egypt. This 6th century figure leads a heavily laden camel and carries the short spear with a massive blade elswhere identified with Arab warriors. He also rides side-saddle! A cavalryman could not fight like this, but it might reflect a riding habit common among camel owners. (Coptic Mus., inv. 8001, Cairo; author's photograph)*

THE OPPOSING PLANS

Initially – before the defeat of the local forces at Ajnadayn – the Byzantines relied on a traditional defensive system to confine and repel the invaders; after Ajnadayn the Byzantine strategy would revert to passive reliance on fortified towns, avoidance of major battles and the use of natural barriers such as rivers and dry valleys. But some fortifications would not be strong enough to resist a determined attack without the support of the mobile forces, dispersed at Ajnadayn. Meanwhile, the Byzantine authorities hoped that the Muslim invaders would weary, as previous desert raiders had done. The fact that these invaders did not do so resulted from the greater commitment provided by their new Muslim religion – a factor the Byzantines failed to recognize.

When the Muslim Arab threat failed to evaporate, Heraclius mustered a very large army to drive them out by force. This had no difficulty in rolling the invaders back from northern and central Syria. The great Byzantine army then established a base near Yaqusah, close to the edge of the Golan Heights, protecting the vital main road from Egypt to Damascus. The base was protected by deep valleys and precipitous cliffs, well supplied with water and grazing. This area lay at the heart of Bilad al Sham, the land of 'Greater Syria', and was important enough for both sides to risk a major battle. But the Byzantines delayed committing themselves, perhaps hoping to undermine the enemy by negotiation in time-honoured Byzantine fashion. When at last the Byzantines did make their move they probably did so after realizing that the Muslims were growing stronger, not weaker. Their main effort was then directed towards the invaders' encampments.

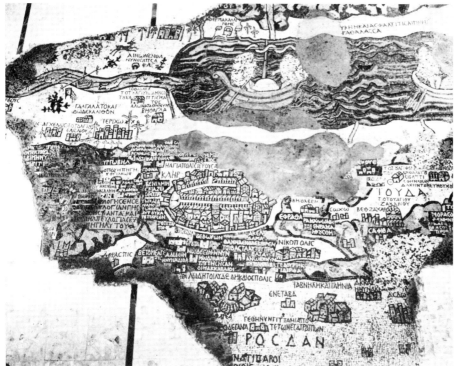

◀ *The famous mid-6th century 'Jerusalem Map' at Madaba shows the fortified Holy City and its surroundings including the Dead Sea. The figures in the two little ships have been obliterated during a period of iconoclastic ('image-hating') fervour during the early 8th century. (in situ, Greek Orthodox Church of St. George, Madaba, Jordan)*

▶ This bronze lamp in the shape of a ship was lost during the Second World War. It comes from 4th–6th century Egypt and has holders for six wicks, three on each side. The ship itself has a ram and several oarsmen, but the most interesting feature is the double stern-post, a feature not otherwise seen until the Middle Ages. This vessel may be an early example of a military transport that could disembark horses from its stern. (Staatliche Museen zu Berlin)

The Muslim Arabs, despite defeating the local Byzantine forces at Ajnadayn, had to take the fortified towns or lose the war. Yet at first they avoided large cities and major Byzantine forces. 'Umar wanted to win over the powerful Syrian tribes before attempting anything more ambitious. Only then would Muslim strategy change. In this second phase, the Caliph's armies would aim at the great cities themselves, most notably Damascus and Emesa (Hims). Unlike the Byzantines, the Muslims then looked for a decisive battle.

Throughout the campaign the Arabs used ruses and ambushes to draw their enemy into the open, almost always successfully. This was to be very obvious in the great battle of Yarmuk itself, where the Muslim Arabs, having studied the ground in detail, would lure the Byzantines into a series of costly assaults before turning the deep valleys and cliffs into a catastrophic trap.

THE CAMPAIGN

Ajnadayn, Pella and Damascus

Ajnadayn was to be the first large battle between Muslim and Christian armies. The Muslim Arab armies are said to have set out from Madina early in 634 but are more likely to have left the previous autumn. After some raiding, their first serious clash with Byzantine troops occurred at Dathin, near Ghazzah, on 4 February. The Emperor Heraclius, then at Emesa, now sent a substantial force to Caesarea Maritima, the main military base in Palestine, where it probably joined units already stationed in the area. A Byzantine fleet also seems to have sailed down the coast in support. The Muslim commanders in southern Palestine in turn requested reinforcements.

Khalid Ibn al Walid had been operating in Iraq and was now ordered to cross the desert to Syria. He arrived in the Damascus area with a small élite unit to defeat a local force of Ghassanid auxiliaries at Easter, 24 April 634. Khalid's desert march caught the imagination of all chroniclers, but its details remain confused and there is still debate about the exact route. Nevertheless, Khalid entered Syria behind the main Byzantine defending forces, taking the strategic fortified town of Busra almost without a fight.

Khalid's force was small, only 500–800 men, but it consisted of troops whose loyalty to Islam was absolute. They seem to have been fast-moving camel-riding infantry with a few cavalry, and their arrival instigated a new phase in the conquest of Syria. Next they joined the forces of Yazid and Shurabil operating east of the Jordan valley and together marched to a pre-arranged mustering in the Wadi Simt, linking up with the army of 'Amr Ibn al As operating in southern Palestine at a place that came to be known as Ajnadayn.

The Byzantines, despite being very close to their own lines of communication, took two months to gather their troops but were still caught unawares by the biggest Muslim army yet assembled against

◀ *The city of Busra in southern Syria stood at the northern end of the ancient trade route to Arabia and was also a vital source of water for desert caravans. This huge reservoir collects rain-water from a wide area. It was originally built by the Romans and has been maintained in perfect working order ever since. (Author's photograph)*

Events from Winter 633 to the end of May 634

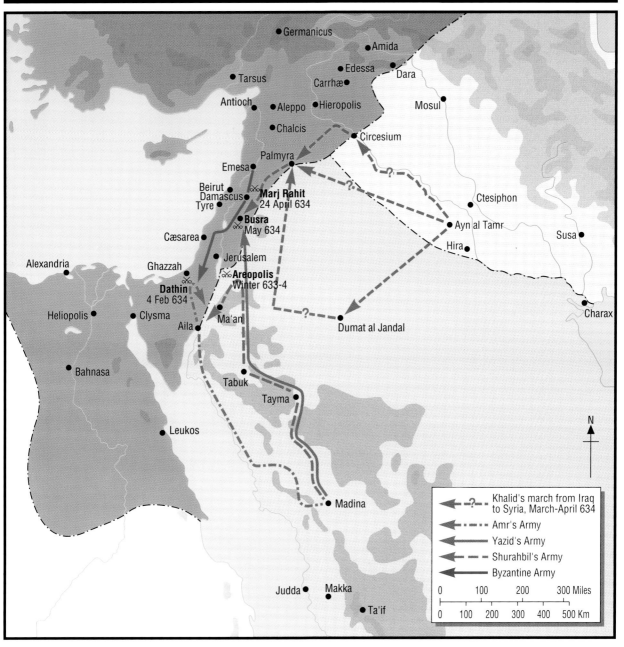

them. Here a road from the Mediterranean to Jerusalem ran thought the Wadi Simt valley, which was moderately broad with sloping, though not precipitous, sides. The battle probably took place west of Bayt Natif, close to the twin villages of Jannaba East and Jannaba West, in July or August 634. The Muslims may have adopted a defensive position west of Bayt Natif, where the road crossed the dry bed of the River Simt. The Byzantine army, led by Heraclius's brother Theodore, expected the support of local Arab auxiliaries but received very little. The Byzantine force may have included the Caesarea garrison under that city's military governor, Sergius, but other chronicles suggest that this Sergius had been killed in February. There is also confusion about an officer named Vardan, who

◄ Khalid Ibn al Walid, hurrying from northern Jordan to reinforce 'Amr Ibn al As in southern Palestine before the battle of Ajnadayn, may have marched down this steep and rugged valley, the Wadi Karak. He would then have gone around the southern end of the Dead Sea, which is visible in the distance. (Author's photograph)

is said to have been at Ajnadayn; but he may have been one and the same as Sergius. The name Vardan itself suggests an Armenian origin. One officer killed at Ajnadayn held the senior rank of *Cubicularius* or perhaps *Sakellarios* and seems to have been Theodore's deputy commander.

Very few hard facts are known about this battle, which is shrouded in pious legend. The Muslims, commanded either by 'Amr Ibn al As or by Khalid Ibn al Walid, decided to meet the Byzantines head-on for the first time. The result was a hard-fought battle without much manoeuvring but with high casualties on both sides. The most convincing, though still hypothetical, reconstruction runs as follows.

Both armies were arrayed in extended lines, with their camps to the rear. The Muslims, and almost certainly the Byzantines, were divided into three divisions with a flank guard on each wing. Mu'az Ibn Jabal commanded the Muslim centre; Sa'id Ibn 'Amir the left; 'Abd al Rahman, son of the Caliph Abu Bakr, the right. Shurahbil led the vital left flank guard, but the name of the man who led the right flank guard is unknown. Behind the centre, protecting the Muslim camp, a reserve was led by Yazid. Khalid, 'Amr and other senior leaders and 'champions' remained near the centre. The Muslims were instructed to shoot showers of arrows as units, not individually, and the women were also

told to defend the camp should the need arise.

Khalid and the Byzantine commander made morale-boosting speeches, the surviving texts of which are almost certainly apocryphal. The exploits of several individuals from each of the armies recorded in Arab chronicles probably recall real events in exaggerated form. A Christian Arab, for example, was sent by the Byzantines to spy on the Muslim camp, coming back with glowing reports of the enemy's morale. A Christian bishop in a black hat tried to negotiate a Muslim withdrawal, to which Khalid replied by offering the traditional choice of conversion to Islam, payment of *jizyah* (tax) or battle. A young Muslim named Zarrar Ibn al Azwar, first recorded as a tax collector at the outbreak of the Riddah Wars, was already known as a fine warrior; he made a reconnaissance of the Byzantine position but, instead of riding straight back as Khalid ordered, turned on his Byzantine pursuers and slew several.

The battle itself began with a barrage of arrows and sling-stones from units stationed ahead of the main Byzantine army. The Muslims were not permitted to reply, but one warrior was sent forward, presumably to maintain Muslim morale. Again it was Zarrar. He is likely to have been the leader of a group of élite champions rather than taking on the Byzantines alone. Normally he fought unarmoured, becoming known as 'The Naked

▶ *The well preserved 6th century Syrian 'Vienna Genesis' includes several interesting military details. 'Esau' or 'Jacob' looks much like any member of a Byzantine army supply train. His mule has a typical pack saddle of a type that would still appear seven centuries later in Islamic manuscripts.*

◀ *A Biblical ruler is protected by two guardsmen dressed and equipped in typical early Byzantine fashion. Mid-length hair was common among the military, and one soldier also has a torque around his neck indicating élite status. (Nat. Bib., Ms. Theol. Gr. 13, Vienna)*

Warrior', but this time he wore a helmet and mail hauberk against the enemy's arrows and carried an 'elephant-hide' shield taken from a Byzantine soldier. After shouting his battle-cry: 'I am the death of the Pale Faces, I am the killer of Romans; I am the scourge sent upon you, I am Zarrar Ibn al Azwar.' He reportedly slew several Byzantine champions including the governors of Amman and Tiberius.

The Muslim army made its attack while these duels were still taking place, and fighting then continued until dusk. Next day the Byzantine commander arranged a parley with Khalid and planned to have the Muslim leader assassinated by a group of hidden soldiers. But the plan went wrong and the leader of the Byzantine party was himself killed, apparently by the fearsome Zarrar. Exploiting the confusion that ensued, the Muslims promptly attacked, and after savage fighting Khalid sent in the reserves under Yazid. The Byzantine line collapsed. The *Cubicularius* was found in the centre, his head wrapped in a cloth, and was killed – according to the Muslim historian al Tabari, the *Cubicularius* had covered his head because he could not bear to witness the carnage around him. More likely he had been wounded.

More 'Companions' and other leading Muslim figures fell at Ajnadayn than in any other battle during the conquest of Syria. Five and a half centuries later there were still many tombs dotted around Wadi Simt and neighbouring hills. The Emperor Heraclius sent his brother Theodore back to Constantinople in disgrace, replacing him with Theodore Trithourios, the *Sakellarios*. The

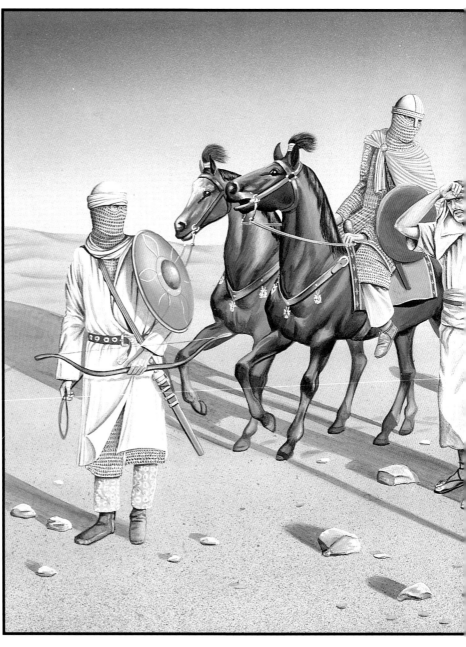

▶ Khalid Ibn al Walid's desert march from Iraq to Syria caught the imagination of early Islamic chroniclers. But even his small force of a few hundred élite **muhajirun** *and* **ansar** *troops had difficulty carrying enough water for the journey. To solve this problem a few camels were denied water to make them exceptionally thirsty; then they were allowed to drink until their bellies were full. These 'living water containers' were slaughtered one by one as the men marched across the worst stretches of desert.*

Byzantines suffered large casualties at Ajnadayn, but the bulk of the shattered army escaped, fleeing to the walled cities. From then on, the Byzantines were wary about facing Muslim forces in the open, while the latter raided far and wide. After the nearby town of Bethlehem fell to the invader, the Patriarch Sophronius of Jerusalem railed against 'the sword of the Saracens... beastly and barbarous... and filled with every diabolic savagery'. Meanwhile the Muslims took a more practical view of their success and even tried to sell their booty back to the

Byzantines! This the Emperor Heraclius angrily refused. He wanted revenge. Meanwhile 'Amr Ibn al As took over a large estate near Bayt Jibrin, not far from Ajnadayn. This he named after one of his followers, 'Ajlan, who may have fallen in the battle.

News of the Battle of Ajnadayn reached the Caliph Abu Bakr on his deathbed. By then many Byzantine cities were crowded with demoralized refugees. Muslim forces strengthened their hold over the countryside, though avoiding the coast, which was vulnerable to counter-attack from the

sea. On the other side the Byzantines still expected these Arab raiders to return to the desert and relied on defensive strategy.

The following months saw blockades, negotiations, raids and secret communication between Muslim leaders, Byzantine commanders and city notables but no major assaults against walled defences. Meanwhile Heraclius was not as apathetic as some of his critics maintained. He sent letters to the main cities reminding the people of Byzantium's recent victories over the Sassanian Empire. He also moved to Antioch, away from vulnerable Emesa. There he set about raising a large army. Heraclius appointed new field and garrison commanders, but many of these newcomers lacked local knowledge, causing friction with the indigenous people. The fortifications of Ghazzah, Ba'albakk and perhaps other places were strengthened, and there seems to have been a militarization of urban leadership.

The Muslim armies had split up after their victory at Ajnadayn, a substantial force under

◀ The battle of Ajnadayn probably took place near the now-deserted Arab village of Bayt Natif where the Roman road crossed the Wadi Simt. The valley also narrows at this point, making it a natural defensive position for the Muslim army. This picture is taken from the ruined tomb of Shaykh Abu Hilal, looking north-west along the Wadi Simt, the direction from which the Byzantines would have advanced. (Author's photograph)

◀ The modern Israeli settlement of Netiv ha Lamed He stands next to the point where the ancient Roman road crossed the Wadi Simt. The Muslim army led by 'Amr Ibn al As and Khalid Ibn al Walid is most likely to have taken up a defensive position across the valley at this point. (Author's photograph)

◀ Below: Ancient Pella lay on the northern side of the little Wadi Jirm, which runs down to the Jordan, seen here looking westward from Tal al Husn on the southern side of the Wadi Jirm. Some ruins can be seen on a bare hillside to the right. Beyond the intensively cultivated Jordan valley rise the hills of Palestine. Baisan, the old Roman city of Scythopolis, lies to the left of the two cloud-shadowed hills in the distance. The battle of Pella took place between Baisan and the Jordan, in an area which was still marshy until modern irrigation schemes altered the area. (Author's photograph)

▶ *A soldier equipped in Byzantine style and with a massive round shield stands guard on a Coptic* ivory situla *made in the 6th century. (British Mus., no. 267, London)*

Khalid Ibn al Walid pursuing the enemy northwards. Many Byzantine troops retreated to Pella (Fihl) and Scythopolis (Baisan) in the Jordan valley, where, according to Muslim sources, they were led by 'the son of Mikhraq, a *Sakellarios*'. These reinforced positions could have formed part of a new defensive line Heraclius is understood to have been organizing. Its eastern flank rested on the Jabal al 'Arab hills, and it would have hemmed the invaders on to the plateau of what is now Jordan. Even here, however, the Muslims had only won control of the flat south and centre of the country, the 'Ajlun hills and the southern part of the Hawran still being in Byzantine hands. The Byzantines'

opening of irrigation canals to create a flooded area in the Jordan valley would fit such an interpretation, as the flat valley floor could have been a weak point in the Byzantine front.

Meanwhile a small detachment of Muslim cavalry led by Abu 'Awar was watching developments at Pella until the main Muslim Arab army arrived. At some stage before the battle of Pella, Khalid Ibn al Walid was removed from command of the Muslim forces in Syria by the new Caliph 'Umar. He was replaced by the pious Abu 'Ubaida, who may have given command of the force outside Pella to Shurahbil. Nevertheless the redoubtable Khalid still apparently led the advance

▶ *Looking down on the ruins of ancient Pella from the citadel of Tal al Husn, where a Byzantine garrison held out for a short while. (Author's photograph)*

guard. And meanwhile Yazid's troops watched the Byzantines in the Yarmuk area.

Shurahbil's army probably advanced from the south-east, where most of the plateau was in Muslim hands, perhaps marching up the eastern side of the Jordan. The Byzantines may have evacuated the town of Pella but are unlikely to have abandoned its powerful citadel. Shurahbil clearly found the flooded area a problem. Winter in this area can be wet and dismal, the Jordan briefly becoming a respectable river instead of a sluggish stream, and even Zarrar failed to get his élite cavalry through the mud. A week later, on 23 January 635, the Byzantine garrison at Scythopolis made an unexpected sortie after sunset, wending through the marshes without difficulty. A desperate battle raged through the night and the following day as the Byzantines hurled themselves at the Muslims' defensive position at the foot of the hills outside Pella. The *Sakellarios* was killed and, as darkness fell again, the Byzantines withdrew. Shurahbil now ordered a counter-attack and the result was carnage as the Byzantines tried to escape back across the marshes and the River Jordan. This 'Battle of Mud' was another disaster for Byzantium. Scythopolis itself surrendered after an unsuccessful sortie, and the garrison above Pella held out for a while before surrendering on generous terms. Shurahbil next took the fortified town of Tiberius before returning south to overrun Byzantine territory in the Balqa

◀ *Another huntsman on the Qusayr 'Amra wall paintings finishes off a fallen animal with a thrust from a spear. (in situ, Qusayr 'Amra, Jordan; author's photographs)*

▼ *Parts of the floor of the Jordan valley were marsh in the 7th century, but these have now been reclaimed to form the most fertile parts of Jordan. Here, looking northwards, the hills of northern Jordan rise on the right. (Author's photograph)*

Events from July 634 to September 635

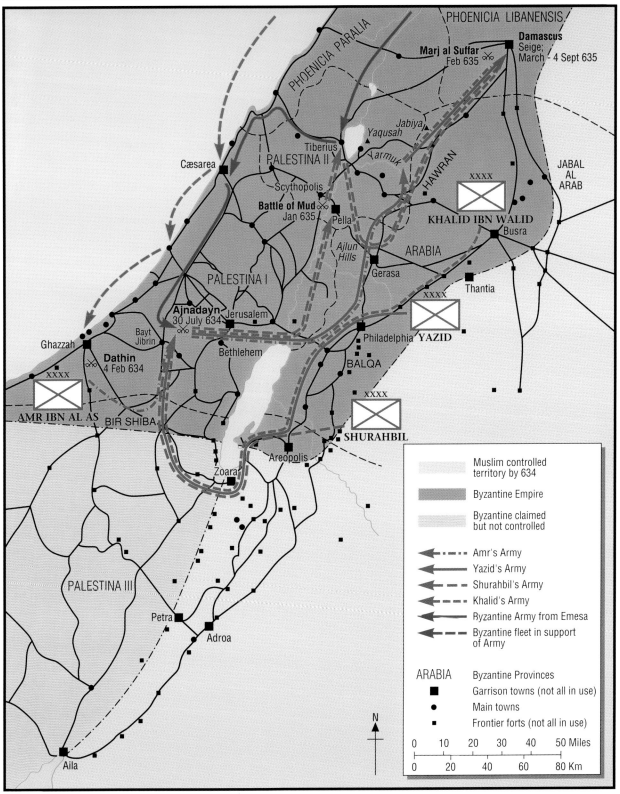

PHOENICIA LIBANENSIS.

PHOENICIA PARALIA

Damascus
Seige;
March - 4 Sept 635

Marj al Suffar
Feb 635

Jabiya

Yaqusah

Tiberius

PALESTINA II

Yarmuk

HAWRAN

JABAL
AL
ARAB

Cæsarea

Scythopolis

Battle of Mud
Jan 635

Pella

Ajlun
Hills

XXXX

KHALID IBN WALID

Busra

ARABIA

PALESTINA I

Gerasa

Thantia

Ajnadayn
30 July 634

Jerusalem

XXXX

Bayt
Jibrin

Philadelphia **YAZID**

Bethlehem

BALQA

Ghazzah

Dathin
4 Feb 634

XXXX

XXXX

AMR IBN AL AS   BIR SHIBA

SHURAHBIL

Areopolis

Zoara

PALESTINA III

Petra

Adroa

Aila

	Muslim controlled territory by 634
	Byzantine Empire
	Byzantine claimed but not controlled
	Amr's Army
	Yazid's Army
	Shurahbil's Army
	Khalid's Army
	Byzantine Army from Emesa
	Byzantine fleet in support of Army

ARABIA   Byzantine Provinces

■   Garrison towns (not all in use)

●   Main towns

▪   Frontier forts (not all in use)

N

| 0 | 10 | 20 | 30 | 40 | 50 Miles |
| 0 | 20 | 40 | 60 | 80 Km |

◀ *The snow-capped peaks of Jabal al Shaykh, Mount Hermon, seen in winter from the area of Marj al Suffar, south of Damascus. This fertile district lies around modern Kiswah, where the old road crossed the river 'Awaj. The Byzantines hoped to halt the Muslim advance at this river crossing, resulting in the battle of Marj al Suffar. (Author's photograph)*

◀ *The inside of the Bab Sharqi or Eastern Gate of Damascus, at the end of the 'Street Called Straight'. This gate appears to have been of the old-fashioned Roman 'straight through' type when the Muslim Arabs beseiged Damascus in 635. Khalid Ibn al Walid's men entered near the Bab Sharqi, while other Muslim forces broke in on the west side of the city. (Author's photograph)*

and southern Hawran region, apparently without resistance.

Meanwhile Heraclius had tried to establish a line along the Yarmuk valley with a base camp near Yaqusah, perhaps the same position as he was to select during the subsequent Yarmuk campaign. But this line was soon breached. The fall of Busra back in May had weakened its eastern flank, the fall of Tiberius now turned its western flank, and a clash seems to have taken place at Marj al Suffar, well to the north of the Yarmuk.

Marj al Suffar, the 'Golden Meadow', was an area of good grazing and abundant water halfway between Damascus and the fertile Ghassanid camping ground at Jabiya on the Golan plateau. It was an ideal base area, particularly in early spring

when the new grass was at its best. But the battle or battles of Marj al Suffar are again shrouded in legend. The main clash may have started when a Muslim advance party under Khalid Ibn Sa'id clashed with a Byzantine force near some water mills, probably on a small ridge south of a stream that runs south of the little town of Kiswah. The Byzantines were probably commanded by a *drungarios*, perhaps one of two Byzantine officers recalled in Arabic as Kulus and Azazir. With water and forage available, and a hill and a river on which to anchor their position, this would have been an obvious place for the Byzantines to defend the approaches to Damascus. Khalid Ibn Sa'id, married the evening before the battle, was killed during the fight; on hearing of his death, his new wife, Umm

Hakim, siezed a tent pole and joined the battle with the perfumed saffron wedding ointment still on her face. The bridge over the stream was thereafter named after Umm Hakim, while the tomb of Khalid Ibn Sa'id stood nearby for centuries.

What happened next is even less clear. Further Muslim units may have arrived and attacked one by one. Khalid Ibn al Walid, Zarrar, Shurahbil and other leaders led their men in repeated *karr wa farr* attacks until the outcome was decided, when Abu 'Ubaida and 'Amr Ibn al As arrived on the scene. Thereupon the Byzantines retired in good order to Damascus, though not before the Byzantine officers Kulus and Azazir had been captured.

The Muslim armies promptly pushed on to Damascus. The Christian Arab Ghassanids may have tried to defend the city from outside the walls, basing their operations on a fortified tower north of the city and awaiting a Byzantine relief force. The entire circuit of walls around Damascus is said to have been manned, though this seems unlikely. A certain Thomas supposedly commanded the garrison and the senior civilian official was Mansur Ibn Sarjan, the Christian Arab financial administrator. He was regarded as a political opponent of the Emperor, probably on religious grounds, and was an ally of the Syriac, rather than Greek Orthodox, bishop.

The siege lasted about six months. Since they were too few to surround Damascus, the Muslims stationed themselves outside each of its gates to impose a blockade. Khalid Ibn al Walid's men faced the East Gate, 'Amr Ibn al As the Gate of Thomas, Abu 'Ubaida the Jabiya Gate, Shurahbil the

▲▶ 'The Siege of the Citadel of Faith', a Coptic wood carving of the 5th–7th centuries. This magnificent object, which was destroyed during the Second World War, portrayed Christian soldiers and enemy horsemen based on Persians or possibly early Muslim Arabs. Above, the 'faithful' come out of the citadel gate, while 'infidel' cavalry ride past, some in mail hauberks, one at least in scale armour. On the right, infantry line the top of the citadel wall. (ex-Kaiser Friedrich Mus., Berlin)

The Siege and Capture of Damascus, March to September 635

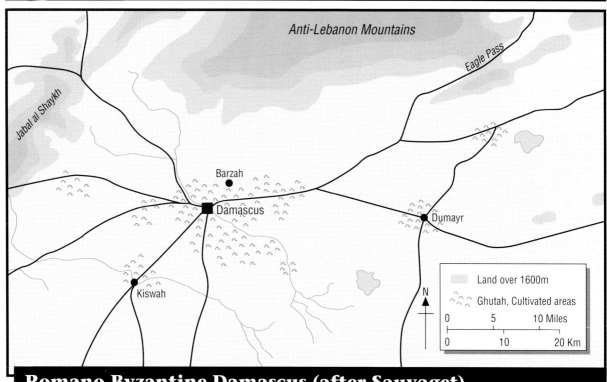

Romano-Byzantine Damascus (after Sauvaget)

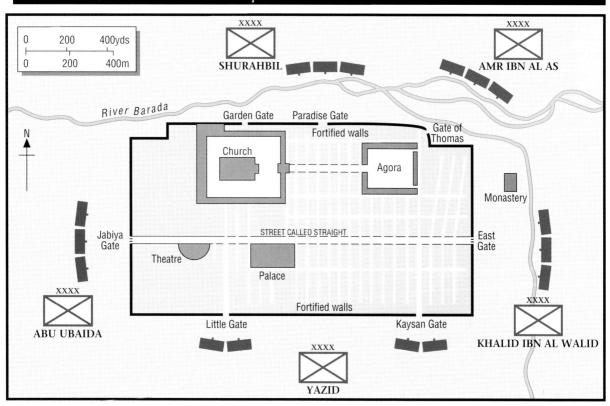

▶ *The old Romano-Byzantine doorway still exists in the southern wall of what became the Great Umayyad Mosque of Damascus, though it is now blocked. For many years Muslims and Christians shared what had once been a huge pagan temple in the heart of the city. Both entered by this door, the Christians turning left to reach their church, the Muslims turning right to reach the section taken as a mosque. (Author's photograph)*

Paradise Gate, and Yazid both the Little and Kaysan Gates. Khalid's headquarters were in a monastery, where the monks tended wounded Muslim soldiers. The infantry engaged any Byzantine troops who appeared on the battlements and faced any sorties, while Muslim women also took up bows to harass the garrison.

Khalid apparently grouped all available cavalry in one force, an important part of which was sent to Thaniyat al 'Uqab ('Eagle's Pass'), where the road from Emesa crossed a spur of the Anti-Lebanon mountains. There they watched for any Byzantine relieving army. A small fort may also have been erected or repaired north of the city at Barzah. One column of Byzantine cavalry was driven back, but again the records are conflicting. The heroic Zarrar Ibn al Azwar was apparently wounded and captured at 'Eagle's Pass'. Khalid Ibn al Walid led his cavalry to help Zarrar's second in command, Rafah Ibn 'Umayrah, who had fallen back towards Bayt Lihya in the Ghutah or 'oasis' of Damascus. As Khalid's troops hurried into battle, a young Arab dressed in black with a green headcloth hiding his face, and armed with spear and sword, galloped past and hurled himself at the Byzantines. The masked rider revived the tired Muslims with his skill and courage, but in the process was unmasked, proving to be Zarrar's sister, Khaula Bint al Azwar, who was fighting to free her brother. Zarrar was in fact freed

as the Muslims pursued the Byzantines towards Emesa where, according to some sources, they were in turn forced back.

The failure of this relief attempt naturally weakened the garrison's morale, which was further jolted by the Muslims' beheading of the two senior officers captured at Marj al Suffar. Several sorties were attempted, and during one of these the garrison commander, Thomas, was wounded in the eye by an arrow shot by the widow of an Arab soldier killed in a previous sortie. The Arab records are generous in their admiration for brave enemies, recording how Thomas led his men in a further sortie during which he almost killed Shurahbil.

Traditional Muslim Arab sources often focus on the personal details of these epic events, and since the medieval Arabs virtually invented the concept of 'romantic love' – a feature notably lacking from Greek and Roman literature – it is not surprising to find that the fall of the city involved a young man known only as 'Jonah the Lover'. This Jonah, son of Marcus, was apparently a Greek whose marriage had been interrupted by the siege. His young wife's parents now claimed to be too busy to finalize the ceremony. Eventually the frustrated Jonah climbed over the wall and offered to give Khalid useful information in return for the Muslim's help in obtaining his bride. Jonah told him that on the night of 18 September there would be a religious festival

◀ *A number of warrior saints appear in fragments of Coptic manuscripts. This illustration of St. Menas shows him in a stylized, very long Arab-style mail hauberk with the neck torque of a senior* *Byzantine officer. The manuscript probably dates from the 6th to 8th century but could be a little later. (John Rylands Lib., Ms. S.33, Manchester)*

Byzantine authorities were negotiating a peaceful surrender with Abu 'Ubaida on the western side of the city and that, on hearing of the break-in to the east, they accepted Abu 'Ubaida's terms and opened the western gates. As a result two Muslim units met in the *macella* (covered market) in the centre of Damascus, where they argued as to whether the city had fallen through negotiation or by force. Nevertheless it was Khalid who drew up the surrender document of 4 September 635, which was endorsed by Abu 'Ubaida. This was generous to the defeated Christians, and only the *Rumi*, or Greeks of Byzantine origin, were excluded from an amnesty.

in the city and only a few sentries would be at their posts. Ropes were brought, ladders borrowed from the neighbouring monastery, an assault party selected and the defences were breached without difficulty.

Other versions state that a messenger from the anti-Byzantine Syriac bishop or from Mansur Ibn Sarjan gave Khalid this information; others that the

The courageous Thomas was killed as the retreating Byzantines were chivvied northwards, and during the chase Jonah the Lover found his bride. But the girl killed herself rather than accept a man who had betrayed his Christian friends. Jonah vowed never to look at another woman and fought on, dying for his new faith at the battle of Yarmuk.

◀ *Not much remains of the citadel of Hims (ancient Emesa), apart from the ruins of some medieval walls and towers. In Byzantine times it was a vital strategic base. (Author's photograph)*

▲ *The fertile Golan plateau was once called the 'bread-basket of Damascus'. It is now sparsely inhabited, but the deserted ruins of many Syrian villages are still linked by roads that follow those laid down by the Romans almost two thousand years ago. This stretch formed one branch of the vital strategic route between Damascus and Egypt. Another ran a little to the south, the two joining near a hill in the distance. The Golan plateau is dotted with many volcanic hillocks, which have played a key role in many conflicts from the Muslim conquest of Syria to the Arab–Israeli war of 1973. (Author's photograph)*

Yazid Ibn Abu Sufyan was left in charge of Damascus while a Muslim army crossed the mountains into the Biqa' valley of central Lebanon, where Heliopolis (Ba'albakk) surrendered, then headed north along the Orontes to take Emesa in November – though this may have capitulated to another column arriving via the 'Eagle's Pass'. Hamah, Shayzar, 'Afa'mi'yah and perhaps Ma'arat al Nu'man fell as the Muslims pressed northwards, the Byzantines retaining Aleppo, Chalcis, most of the coastal strip and of course Antioch, where Heraclius had made his military headquarters. Generally speaking, the Muslims were greeted as liberators, particularly in the countryside. Other units mopped up enemy outposts in southern Syria, Jordan and Palestine.

The Byzantine Counter-Attack

The Byzantine Emperor Heraclius could not admit defeat in Syria: indeed, a century would pass before the Empire came to accept the loss of these rich provinces. It was several months before Heraclius's newly assembled army could launch a counter-offensive. In addition to élite troops from the capital, it included local forces from lands recently lost to the Muslims as well as Armenians led by a certain Gargis and allied-Arab tribes led by Jabala the Ghassanid. Heraclius himself supervised operations from Antioch, but quite who was in supreme command of the army is unclear. It was probably Vahan the Armenian, recently the commander at Emesa, but divided authority was not unknown in Byzantine military history. Theodore Trithourios the *Sakellarios* may have been joint leader, while Niketas, son of Shahrbaraz, and Jabala the Ghassanid were probably subordinates. For the first time, Byzantine forces in Syria greatly outnumbered the Muslims.

Faced with such a massive counter-stroke, Abu 'Ubaida followed Khalid's advice, and the Muslims

kilometres wide. It is also said to have been protected by a ditch.

It has been suggested that Vahan chose this strong base to give his men time to get acclimatized; it is more likely that he wanted to protect the vital road between Syria and Byzantine-held Egypt, which also ran across this 'peninsula', while at the same time threatening Muslim-held Jordan. Both sides had access to fodder for their animals and adequate water supplies. From a tactical point of view the plateau was good cavalry country, but its many dips, gullies and rocky outcrops also provided good cover for infantry. On the other hand, the Byzantine army was operating in an unfriendly environment. In Damascus, Mansur Ibn Sarjan was accused of inciting the people to make such a din one night that Byzantines thought they were under attack; the soldiers abandoning their positions. Mansur's primary motive may have been to prevent the Byzantines extorting provisions, but one result was to weaken the army's morale. In addition to local Arab tribes and peasants of varied religious affiliations there was a large Jewish population in the villages of Nawa and Dara'ah. The Jewish Arab Banu Nadhir tribe, expelled from the Hijaz by Muhammad in 625, had also settled around Dara'ah. They may have disliked their Muslim fellow Arabs, but they hated Heraclius even more. In 630 the Emperor had decreed that all Jews must become Christian; a massacre followed around Jerusalem and in Galilee, some survivors probably fleeing to the Dara'ah area. It seems that, for a while at least, many Jews thought the Prophet Muhammad was the promised Messiah.

For almost three months the two armies watched each other while the Byzantines tried to subvert the Muslims in their traditional manner. Vahan seems to have opened negotiations through his senior Armenian officer, Gargis (George), and

withdrew to territory of their own choosing. They also returned the taxes they had taken from Emesa because they could not protect it as agreed in the original surrender terms. Damascus was also abandoned. Khalid was recognized as the most able field commander, but Abu 'Ubaida remained in overall strategic command, coordinating various armies and assembling scattered Muslim forces near the River Yarmuk. At first they concentrated at Jabiya, where there was abundant water and pasture. A serious clash occurred, perhaps in mid-July, and the pro-Byzantine Ghassanids forced the Muslims out of Jabiya.

On Khalid's advice they retreated to a position between Dara'ah and Dayr Ayyub, covering the gap between the Yarmuk gorges and the *Harra* lava plain. The advancing Byzantines may first have camped at Kiswah, just south of Damascus, but a strongly fortified base-camp was soon established near Yaqusah. This was an immensely strong position a day and a half's march from Damascus. With the Yarmuk and Ruqqad valleys to the south-east, the barely less precipitous slopes of the Samak valley and Golan Heights to the north-west, it stood on a 'peninsula' of flat land joined to the main Golan plateau by a narrow 'isthmus' less than four

Events from September 635 to August 636

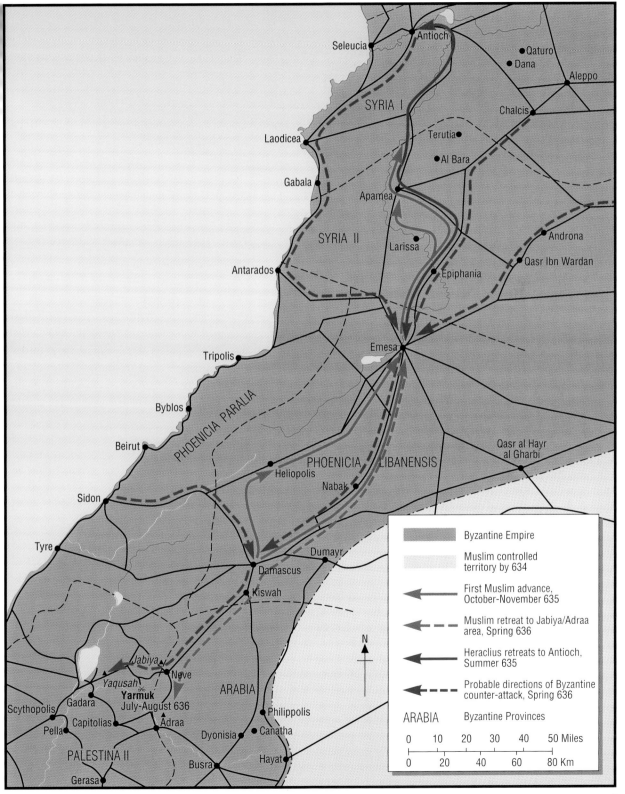

Antioch
Seleucia
Qaturo
Dana
Aleppo
Chalcis
SYRIA I
Laodicea
Terutia
Al Bara
Gabala
Apamea
SYRIA II
Androna
Larissa
Qasr Ibn Wardan
Antarados
Epiphania
Emesa
Tripolis
Byblos
PHOENICIA PARALIA
Beirut
Qasr al Hayr
al Gharbi
PHOENICIA LIBANENSIS
Heliopolis
Nabak
Sidon
Tyre
Dumayr
Damascus
Kiswah

Byzantine Empire

Muslim controlled territory by 634

First Muslim advance, October-November 635

Muslim retreat to Jabiya/Adraa area, Spring 636

Heraclius retreats to Antioch, Summer 635

Probable directions of Byzantine counter-attack, Spring 636

ARABIA   Byzantine Provinces

N

Jabiya
Neve
Yaqusah
Yarmuk
July-August 636
ARABIA
Scythopolis
Gadara
Philippolis
Capitolias
Adraa
Pella
Dyonisia
Canatha
PALESTINA II
Busra
Hayat
Gerasa

0 10 20 30 40 50 Miles
0 20 40 60 80 Km

then via Jabala the Ghassanid. The Muslim Arabs, however, were not interested, and on 23 July they counter-attacked, defeating the troops of Theodore Trithurios and of Jabala to regain Jabiya.

The nature of the terrain was to have a profound effect on this manoeuvring and on the final outcome of the battle. Great gorges cut by the Yarmuk, Ruqqad, 'Allan and Harir rivers are the main features of the area, slicing deep into the level plateau, their edges steep, though not everywhere cliffs. This applies only on the southern part of the plateau. Farther north, seasonal streams run through wadis but a few metres deep. There are also several springs and some areas of marshy ground on the plateau, while isolated hills, the remains of long-dead volcanic eruptions, thrust through the surface. The plateau itself consists of two types of surface: rough areas dotted with boulders and volcanic outcrops, and clear areas that are more intensively cultivated. Many villages now dot the area, as they probably did in the 7th century. Only to the west, in

what is now Israeli-occupied Golan, have these been bulldozed into oblivion.

Ancient ruins going back much earlier are also scattered across the plateau, including pre-Christian temples and a remarkable number of tombs associated with Old Testament Biblical figures. Enoch (Idris) was supposedly born near Tal al Harra, Job (Ayyub) is buried at Dayr Ayyub, Noah's son Shem is buried at Nawa and the prophet Elisha at Busr al Hariri. The Ghassanid 'capital' of Jabiya lay north of the main Roman road, next to the isolated hill of Tal Jabiya. This commands such an important view that it is a sensitive Syrian Army observation position today. Khisfin, with its vast ancient necropolis, lies to the south-west, just inside occupied territory where the number of volcanic hills gets more numerous. Another necropolis lies next to al 'Al close to where the main Byzantine camp was erected. But one of the strangest ancient relics on the battlefield is the Qubur Bani 'Isra'il, 'Tombs of the Israelites', ancient dolmens next to

◀ *A 6th–7th century Christian manuscript from what is now north-eastern Syria shows 'Moses before Pharoah and his guards'. It was made in a war-torn frontier region, so the domed helmet with large cheek-pieces worn by one guard is probably more accurate than helmets shown in manuscripts made in peaceful regions. (Bib. Nat., Ms. Syr. 341, Paris)*

'Ayn Dhakar and the bridge over the Ruqqad, where the fate of the Byzantine army was eventually to be sealed.

There was clearly dissention and indiscipline within the Byzantine ranks before the battle. There may even have been clashes between various units leading to bloodshed, although the story of an Armenian mutiny proclaiming Vahan as Emperor is probably a myth. (There was an Armenian rising against the Emperor Heraclius in 636, but this was by David Saharouni, a quasi-independent prince in eastern Anatolia.) The Armenian division at Yarmuk was commanded by Gargis (George), but one of his senior officers, the *Buccinator*, refused to accept Gargis's orders. To further confuse the issue, the *Buccinator* may also have held the rank of *Drungarios* or have been given command of another division before the main battle. At this stage the Christian Arab auxiliaries included the dominant Ghassan tribe as well as men from the Lakhm, Judham, Bal-Qayn, Bali, Amila and Quda'a tribes. It is interesting to note that the Lakhm, Bali and Judham were also represented in the opposing Muslim Arab army, many of their men still being Christians.

While the Byzantines were weakened by dissent, the Muslims were being reinforced, mostly by Yemeni troops, the bulk of whom seem to have been infantry archers. The Muslim Arab army eventually included men from Yemen, Najran, Hadramawt, Hijaz and Syria. Finally the Byzantines, seeing that the Muslims were growing stronger and having failed to sow dissention among the enemy's leaders, descided to attack. At this point the Muslims were still outnumbered by four to one.

Tented Muslim encampments may have been strung out between Dara'ah and Jabiya to take advantage of a series of springs feeding the many head waters of the River Yarmuk in the hot, dry summer. Quite when Vahan established his forward position near the Wadi 'Allan is not clear; nor is its exact location. Jallin has been suggested but would seem dangerously far forward. It also had steep valleys to the rear, hindering communication with Yaqusah. The Byzantines already seem to have been suffering desertions and, despite the size of his army, Vahan was unable to cover the 'front' between the Yarmuk–'Allan gorges and Roman roads to the

▲ *This clay lamp from Egypt, decorated with the story of David and Goliath, is said to date from the 4th–5th centuries, but aspects of Goliath's arms and* *armour suggest that it was made a century or so later. (Yale Univ. Art Gallery, Gift of Rebecca Darlington Stoddard, 1913, New Haven)*

north. In the meantime Vahan reportedly met Khalid and offered huge sums of money for a Muslim withdrawal, which Khalid refused. Battle was joined the following day.

The Battle of Yarmuk

Vahan commanded 15,000 to 20,000 troops, yet the Byzantine 'front' may also have been up to thirteen kilometres long. Clearly there would have been substantial gaps between Byzantine divisions if Vahan was trying to cover the whole area between the Yarmuk gorge and the Roman roads, and the subsequent struggle may have been a series of almost separate battles between divisions. The right was commanded by Gargis and included heavy infantry with large shields trained to form a shield-wall, a tactic echoed in Arabic accounts in which Gargis's men supposedly 'chained themselves together'. Here, close to the upper Yarmuk valley, the infantry's role was to form an anchor while leaving large-scale manoeuvre to the left wing and perhaps the centre. Vahan himself commanded the centre, largely consisting of Armenian troops, while the *Buccinator* commanded the left. Jabala's Arab auxiliaries were light cavalry, perhaps with some camel-mounted infantry, and they appear in various parts of the battlefield, firstly as scouts or skirmishers ahead of the main army and covering the exposed left flank. Others defended the bridge over the Wadi Ruqqad at 'Ayn Dhakar three or four kilometres to the rear. There was no mention of Theodore Thithurios commanding a division, perhaps because he was an administrative officer.

According to later Armenian sources, the Byzantine army was drawn up in twenty separate units, Vahan stationing himself on a small hill behind the right wing. Identifying this hill would shed considerable light on the position of the Byzantine army. The most obvious candidate is a substantial knoll (500 metres above sea level) south-east of 'Ayn Dhakar. If the Roman road from the Ruqqad bridge to Tsil ran through the centre of the Byzantine 'front' then this knoll would have been slightly to the right. It also commanded a minor junction in the road. It now seems to be called Rujm

al Mushabbah, a name which could be translated as 'The tombs of those who ignited war'. The right wing of Vahan's army, his élite infantry divisions, would have anchored its flank on the point where the Wadi 'Allan dipped down a series of waterfalls into its deep gorge. Behind them was a large open area which, though covered in stones and small volcanic mounds, presented no serious obstacles until the precipitous gorge of the Wadi Ruqqad some four kilometres away. To the south the even deeper valley of the Yarmuk meant that the enemy could not turn this flank. How far Vahan's left flank extended is unclear, but his army outnumbered the Muslims about four to one, so he was confident that he could extend farther than they could. It probably stretched beyond the southern Roman roads as far as the northern Roman road near Jabiya, indicating the tactical importance of Jabiya itself. Farther north lay a large flat, waterless, stony and virtually uninhabited area known as the Jidur, 'the area that looks as if it suffers from small-pox'.

By now the Muslim leaders had a good idea of enemy capabilities. A local tradition stated that the Tal al Jumu'a, one of several hills north of Tsil, was

▲ *The site of the first phase of the battle of Yarmuk, looking north from 'Ayn Habis in Jordan. The Wadi Zayyatin enters the Yarmuk valley from the left, while the Syrian village of Shajarah is in the distance. (Author's photograph)*

◀ *The Wadi Ruqqad seen from its western edge at the site of the destroyed Syrian village of Jibnin. The main battle of Yarmuk was probably fought on the plateau in the distance, but after their left flank was turned the Byzantine troops tried to escape westwards across this deep valley. (Author's photograph)*

where the Muslim army gathered for battle. In fact this was probably where they anchored their right (northern) flank; unless the Byzantines patrolled this area, it could have concealed a substantial force.

Abu 'Ubaida delegated command to Khalid Ibn al Walid, who supposedly divided his troops into thirty-six infantry units forming four divisions. Three cavalry units under Qays Ibn Hubaurah, Maysara Ibn Masruq and 'Amir Ibn Tufayl were placed behind the centre and flank with a larger cavalry reserve in the rear. The Muslim army was probably placed between Saham al Jawlan and Tal al Jabiya, with the Byzantines a kilometre and a half away. Yazid Ibn Abu Sufyan commanded the left flank, Abu Abir 'Amr Ibn al Jara'a the centre, which consisted of Abu 'Ubaida's men on the centre-left, Shurahbil's on the centre-right. 'Amr Ibn al As commanded the right flank. The Muslim archers, mostly Yemenis, were spread along the entire front while Zarrar led the cavalry reserve under Khalid's immediate command.

The location of the Muslim camp has been seen as a problem. In fact there were probably several encampments of separate tribes behind each

▲▼*Arab influence on the Qusayr 'Amra wall-paintings is clearest in a representation of a desert hunt, above . Women peer out from typical bedouin tents, while a bearded man waves flaming torches to frighten the animals into a screened enclosure. Among the ceiling figures, below, is this infantry archer, who uses the Mediterranean finger-draw rather than the more advanced Central Asian thumb-draw. (in situ, Qusayr 'Amra, Jordan; author's photographs)*

▲ *The site of the final phase of the battle of Yarmuk seen from 'Ayn Habis on the southern side of the Yarmuk. Above the cliffs is the south-eastern end of the plateau where the battle ended. Beyond this plateau is the Wadi Ruqqad, on the far side of which rises the slightly higher Golan plateau. (Author's photograph)*

division. These would have occupied the water sources, and provided arrows and other such supplies. A later Armenian chronicler stated that the Muslims hobbled their camels to form a barrier around these camps. Here the women could also tend the wounded.

The battle was a major confrontation lasting six days of hard fighting. The story that a senior Byzantine officer came over to Islam on the morning of the first day, and that he died a martyr shortly afterwards, is probably apochryphal, but it is possible that some Christian Arab auxiliaries changed sides at the last moment. The first day

started with duelling by champions. At noon Vahan sent forward infantry including archers, and hand-to-hand fighting continued until sunset.

Early on the second day the Byzantines advanced along the whole front and caught their enemies at dawn prayers; perhaps having learned something of Muslim culture. Vahan's intention seems to have been to hold the centre while attacking the flanks of his numerically inferior foe. After three such attacks, the Muslim right fell back and Byzantine troops reached one or more of the Arab camps. There the retreating Muslim infantry and cavalry were met by their own womenfolk who

▼ *Arab women took part in several battles during the Muslim conquest of Syria and Palestine, sometimes individually, sometimes defending their*

tents. *The most celebrated occasion was when the fifty-year old Hind, mother of the future Caliph Mu'awiyah and at one time a dedicated opponent of the Prophet Muhammad, led the defence of the Muslim camp following a Byzantine breakthrough during the battle of Yarmuk.*

◀ *Armenian troops played a leading role in 7th century Byzantine armies. A few Armenian carvings survive from this period, including these made around 640 on the outside of the cathedral at Mrèn. This horse shows a transitional form of framed saddle, having a raised pommel at the front but no cantle at the back, a type that also appears in Byzantine and Sassanian art. (in situ, west portal of Mrèn Cathedral, Armenia; N. Thierry photograph)*

abused them for running away, beat drums, threw stones and sang songs to shame the men back into battle.

The same scenario was enacted slightly later on the Muslims' left flank, where the Byzantine infantry had advanced more slowly across the Wadi 'Allan. Here the seventy-three year old Abu Sufyan, once one of the Prophet Muhammad's most dedicated opponents, was fighting as a horseman in the Muslim ranks. As he retreated he encountered his wife, the ferocious, fat and fifty year old Hind Bint 'Utba – a lady of character if unorthodox morals. After forcing Abu Sufyan back into battle with a tent pole, she began singing the same song she sang at the battle of Uhud, when she had once encouraged pagan Arabs fighting against the first Muslims:

'We are the daughters of the night;
We move amongst the cushions,
With the grace of gentle kittens
Our bracelets on our elbows.
If you attack we shall embrace you;
And if you retreat we will forsake you
With a loveless separation.'

It was hardly Islamic, but it worked and the Byzantines were held. Khalid sent the cavalry reserve to support first the right and then the left flank, while the Muslim centre counter-attacked, supported by Zarrar with a squadron of cavalry, and broke through the enemy line at one point. The second day then ended with both armies pulling back to their original positions.

On the third day the Byzantine army attempted a similar attack but concentrated on the open northern flank of the battlefield. Once again 'Amr's men fell back to their tents, along with part of Shurahbil's division. Again the Muslims came up against their own women, one soldier reportedly saying, 'It is easier to face the Rumi [Byzantines] than our wives!' Again the situation was retrieved by Khalid's cavalry reserve, but this time Muslim casualties were much higher.

Precisely when Khalid Ibn al Walid launched his famous flanking movement depends on how the Arabic sources are interpreted. Major General Akram of the Pakistani Army believes that it was on the sixth and final day. Professor Ghawanmi of Jordan's Yarmuk University suggests the third and fourth days. The latter seems most likely, but the

question remains – did Khalid lure the enemy forward into a flanking 'ambush' or did he take advantage of a brief breakdown in Byzantine coordination?

The fourth day was certainly hard fought and decisive. By now the Muslims had lost a great many archers while Vahan, having nearly broken through on the third day, repeated his attack – in fact, the nature of the battlefield meant that he had few other options, despite his numerical superiority. This time the Armenian regiments, supported by the Ghassanid cavalry, drove back Shurahbil's division. In response the divisions of Abu 'Ubaida and Yazid struck at the Byzantine centre and right. Khalid sent half the mobile cavalry reserve to join those already under Qays Ibn Hubayrah and himself took command of the rest. The advancing Armenians and Christian Arabs now found themselves attacked on three sides by Khalid, Shurahbil and Qays. After fierce fighting, the Byzantines retreated, the Ghassanid auxiliaries suffering particularly heavy losses.

Whether or not Khalid's flanking movement was on this fourth day, it is clear what happened. While attacking the northern Muslim encamp-

▲ *Other 7th century Armenian carvings include this portrayal of 'Manuel, lord of the Amatuni family' apparently using stirrups, a more advanced form of saddle and a fully developed composite bow. (in situ, southern window of church, Ptghni, Armenia; Dr. L. Der Manuelian photograph)*

ments, the Byzantine cavalry became separated from its infantry. Perhaps the Byzantines were attempting one of the complex 'mixed formation' manoeuvres described in the *Strategikon* of Maurice; operations that could lead to a gap opening between horse and foot. Being unable to return to the safety of their infantry, the Byzantine cavalry fled north. Khalid's cavalry then attacked the Byzantine's left flank, forcing the *Buccinator's* division and Vahan's Armenians to retreat.

Even more serious were the actions of a small Muslim Arab cavalry unit under Zarrar, which seems to have remained hidden behind Tal al Jumu'a during the initial Byzantine advance. When the Byzantine cavalry fled, Zarrar followed them towards 'Ayn Dhakar. Most of the retreating Byzantine cavalry were Christian Arab auxiliaries of the Lakhm and Judham tribes. Some scattered into

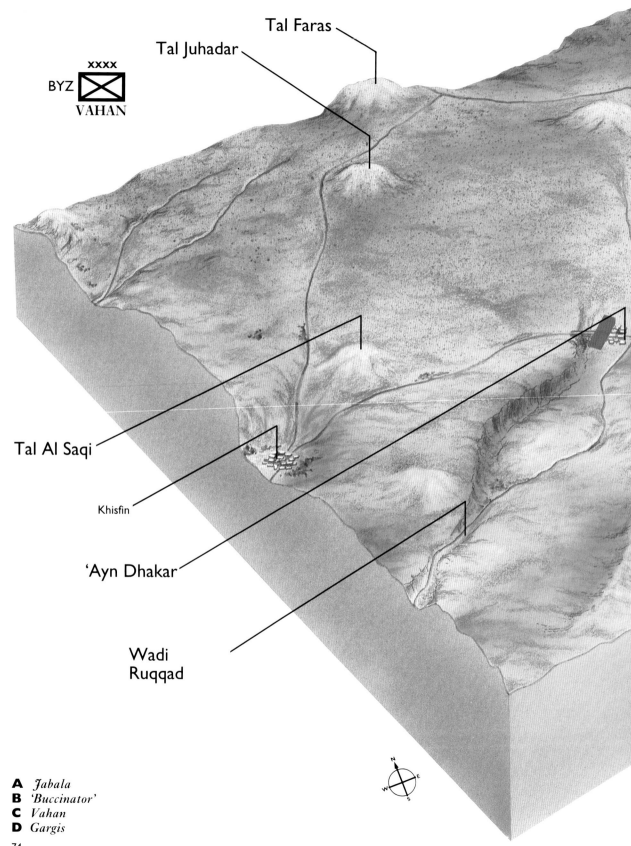

Tal Faras

Tal Juhadar

BYZ **xxxx** VAHAN

Tal Al Saqi

Khisfin

'Ayn Dhakar

Wadi
Ruqqad

N
W E
S

A *Jabala*
B *'Buccinator'*
C *Vahan*
D *Gargis*

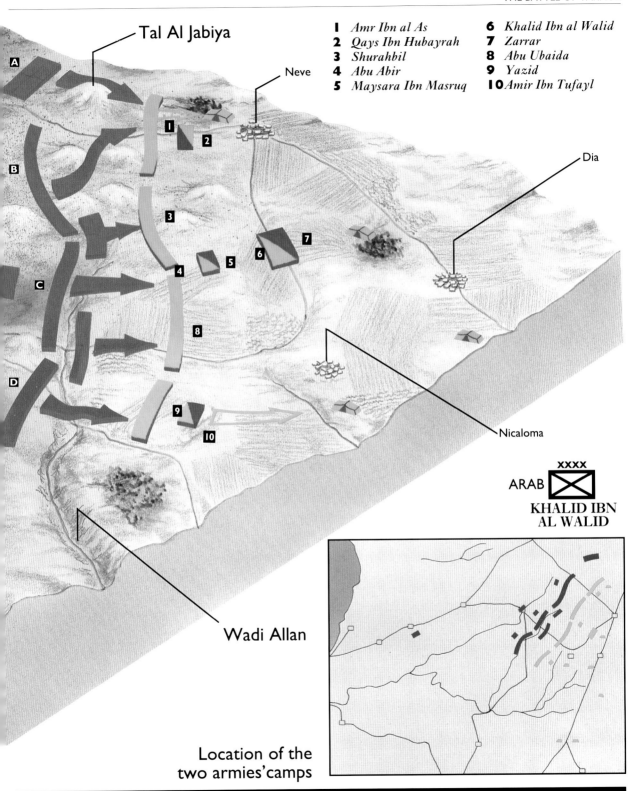

Tal Al Jabiya

Neve

Dia

Nicaloma

1	Amr Ibn al As	6	Khalid Ibn al Walid
2	Qays Ibn Hubayrah	7	Zarrar
3	Shurahbil	8	Abu Ubaida
4	Abu Abir	9	Yazid
5	Maysara Ibn Masruq	10	Amir Ibn Tufayl

ARAB

xxxx

KHALID IBN
AL WALID

Wadi Allan

Location of the
two armies' camps

THE BATTLE OF YARMUK: THE SECOND DAY

Showing the position of the armies at the start of the day, 16 August 636

local villages; some deserted to the Muslims. Their flight infected other Arab auxiliaries guarding the only bridge over the Wadi Ruqqad, and as a result Zarrar, guided by a deserter named Abu Ju'aid, captured the bridge with ease. The Byzantine army was now cut off from its main camp at Yaqusah and could only retreat by scrambling down the Yarmuk or Ruqqad gorges or breaking out northwards – across barren territory through the main Muslim army, which had moved across the Byzantine left flank.

Meanwhile, in the central and southern sectors the Muslims were suffering terribly from Byzantine archery in what became known as 'The Day of Lost Eyes'. Here they were now fighting with virtually no cavalry support, so perhaps these injuries were inflicted by Byzantine horse archers. Abu 'Ubaida and Yazid fell back with the Byzantines close behind, but one Muslim unit on the left edge of Abu 'Ubaida's division, led by Iqrama Ibn Abi Jahl, was cut off. Every man was killed or seriously wounded. This time the Muslim divisions did not

◀ *The Yarmuk gorge looking south-east from the site of the abandoned Syrian village of Yaqusah, traditionally the place where many Byzantine troops fell down cliffs as they fled from the victorious Muslims. Some precipitous cliffs are, in fact, deep in the valley beyond the hill on the right of this picture. (Author's photograph)*

his army's escape – but to no avail. The Byzantines were now penned between the Ruqqad and Yarmuk gorges, separated from their camp at Yaqusah. The Muslims probably occupied a front between the Wadi 'Allan and Wadi Ruqqad. Neither side attacked, perhaps being exhausted by the previous day's combat, but both Khalid and Vahan assembled their remaining cavalry into single units.

Again the exact date on which the Muslims stormed the camp at Yaqusah is unknown, though it seems to have happened at night. Perhaps Zarrar simply pressed on after siezing the bridge, reaching Yaqusah eighteen kilometres away after dark. Finding its defences denuded, the Muslims may have captured it with ease. Those defenders who remained would have fled along the Roman road south-west towards Palestine, but others could have found themselves trapped against the edge of the Ruqqad and Yarmuk gorges. Perhaps some fell down cliffs in the dark, the first to die in this manner at the battle of Yarmuk.

The sixth and final day of the battle began with skirmishing between the formations of Gargis and Abu 'Ubaida, during which Gargis was killed. The entire Muslim army then surged foward. The struggle was fiercest at the north-western end of the front where the Muslims may have been attempting to drive the enemy farther from the bridge. In any event, the *Buccinator's* troops were driven towards Vahan's own division in the centre.

The story that the Byzantines were unsettled or blinded by a sand-storm is almost certainly a myth and only appears as 'a cloud of dust and adverse wind' in a later account by Theophanes, who was trying to explain away the Christian defeat. It also goes against the nature of the terrain and the normal wind direction. Nevertheless the Byzantines were siezed by panic: their escape was cut off. Some laid down their weapons and attempted to surrender, but the Muslims, having

retreat far. Instead the women came forward, led by Zarrar's sister, Khaula Bint al Azwar. One woman was urging the men to cut off the enemies' uncircumcised private parts; some say that it was again the formidable Hind. The Byzantines were driven back, but his time it was Zarrar who ended the day looking for his sister Khaula, finding her among the wounded with a nasty sword cut to the head.

On the fifth day Vahan made a final attempt to negotiate a Muslim withdrawal – or more probably

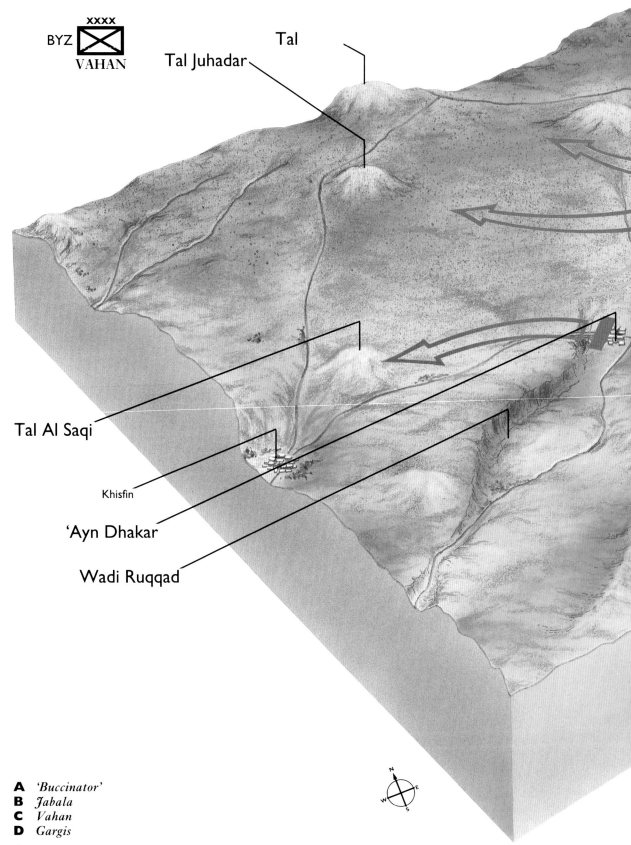

BYZ

xxxx

VAHAN

Tal

Tal Juhadar

Tal Al Saqi

Khisfin

'Ayn Dhakar

Wadi Ruqqad

A   'Buccinator'
B   Jabala
C   Vahan
D   Gargis

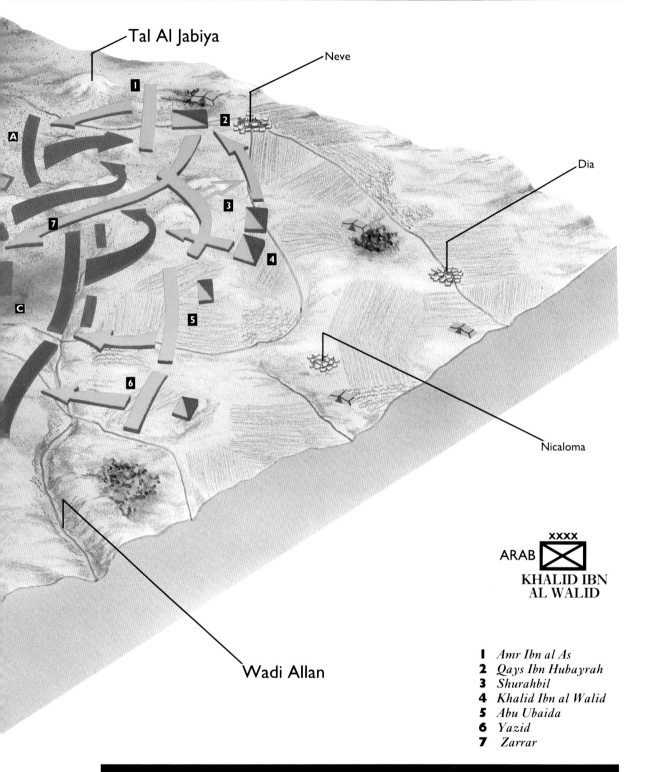

Tal Al Jabiya

Neve

Dia

Nicaloma

Wadi Allan

ARAB

xxxx
KHALID IBN
AL WALID

1 Amr Ibn al As
2 Qays Ibn Hubayrah
3 Shurahbil
4 Khalid Ibn al Walid
5 Abu Ubaida
6 Yazid
7 Zarrar

THE BATTLE OF YARMUK: FOURTH DAY

Showing the Byzantine attacks, the Muslim flanking movement and the seizure of the Wadi Ruqqad bridge

suffered appalling losses, did not take many prisoners. Others tried to escape down the steep slopes and cliffs where some fell to their deaths. These would have been few, but the horror of their fate was given prominence in the early accounts. Most of those who escaped must either have fled along the the valley or clambered up the southern slopes into what is now Jordan.

The aged Abu Sufyan, husband of the redoubtable Hind, was among the many Muslims who lost an eye. A man named Hubash Ibn Qais al Kushairi had part of his foot cut off but did not notice until later, whereupon he started wandering about the battlefield looking for it! 'Amir Ibn Abi Waqqas, who had previously brought 'Umar's orders that Khalid be demoted from senior command, was

THE BATTLE OF YARMUK

killed along with many other highly respected figures listed in the Arab chronicles. The tombs of these leading Muslims were still identifiable in the late 12th century. Some are still visible at al Mahajjah, north of Nawa, and in the ruins of an old Byzantine monastery east of the Damascus– Dara'ah road.

The Muslims' losses were small compared with those of the Byzantines, though thousands of the latter did escape to Emesa and Egypt. Some cavalry, which had fled early on, even tried to slow the Muslim advance northwards. The fate of Byzantine commanders varied. Vahan was either killed on the battlefield or as he fled, or may have escaped to become a monk at St. Catherine's Monastery in Sinai. Theodore Trithurios died in the battle, but Niketas reached Emesa, where he tried to go over to the Muslims but was rejected. Jabala also escaped and was for a while successful in coming to terms with the conquerors.

◀ *The junction of the Wadi Ruqqad on the left, the Yarmuk gorge in the centre, and the Wadi 'Aqraba in Jordan on the right, seen from the abandoned Syrian village of Yaqusah. The Muslims finally trapped the Byzantines on the spur of land between the Ruqqad and the Yarmuk. (Author's photograph)*

▲ *Mounted figures continued to be a popular motif on Egyptian textiles after the Muslim conquest. This 7th or 8th century example includes stirrups, a new idea, which the weaver seems not to have fully understood. (Textile Museum, Washington; author's photograph)*

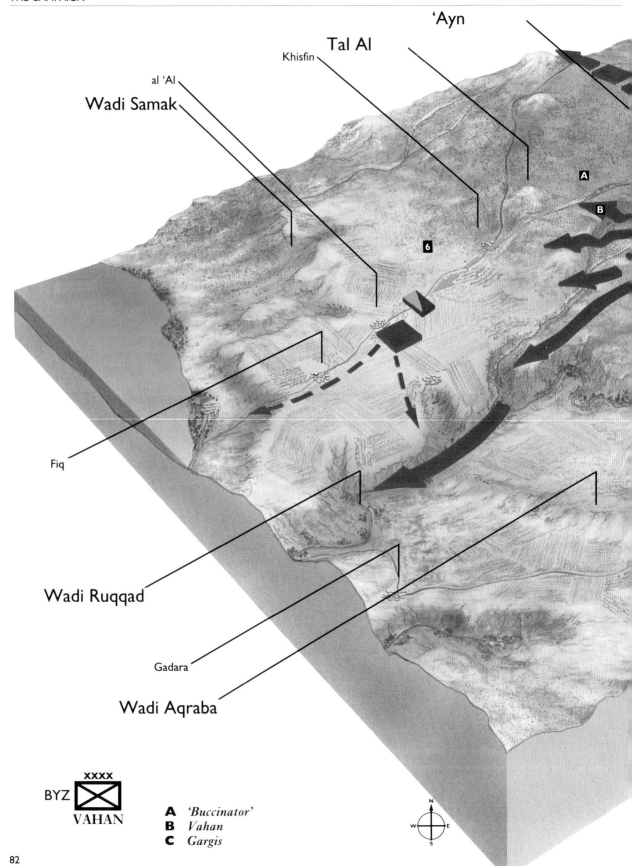

'Ayn

Tal Al

Khisfin

al 'Al

Wadi Samak

A

B

6

Fiq

Wadi Ruqqad

Gadara

Wadi Aqraba

BYZ

XXXX

VAHAN

A *'Buccinator'*
B *Vahan*
C *Gargis*

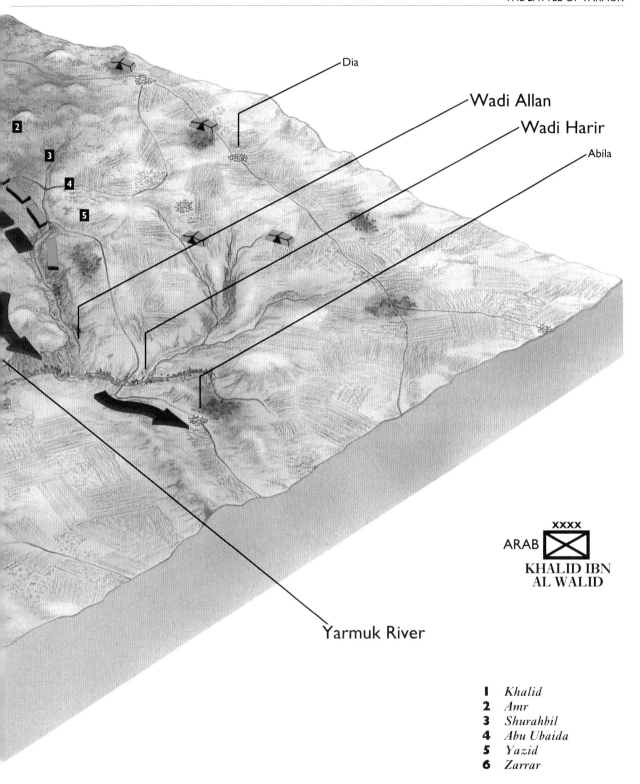

Dia

Wadi Allan

Wadi Harir

Abila

2

3

4

5

ARAB

XXXX

KHALID IBN
AL WALID

Yarmuk River

1   *Khalid*
2   *Amr*
3   *Shurahbil*
4   *Abu Ubaida*
5   *Yazid*
6   *Zarrar*

THE BATTLE OF YARMUK: THE FINAL DAY

Showing the Byzantines collapse, 20 August 636

◄ A strategically important road still climbs these, the southernmost slopes of the Golan Heights, as it has done since the days of the Egyptian Empire. Just beyond trees in the middle distance, vertical cliffs plunge down to the River Yarmuk. Beyond them rises the north-western spur of the Jordanian plateau, the intensively cultivated Jordan valley and, hidden in heat haze, the hills of Palestine. (Author's photograph)

The Fall of Byzantine Syria

Now that the battle was over, Abu 'Ubaida reassumed overall command, putting Habib Ibn Maslamah in charge of the cavalry spearheading the Muslim advance. Damascus surrendered on the same terms that it had accepted the previous year. Mansur Ibn Sarjan was again involved in negotiations as the Byzantine garrison departed. Yazid was left to govern Damascus, while Khalid and Abu 'Ubaida continued northwards.

Since they had not contemplated defeat, the Byzantines had no fall-back position, and large numbers of soldiers retreated into Anatolia to avoid being cut off. Meanwhile the Muslims retook Emesa. In some areas they were greeted with songs and dancing, but in northern Syria Byzantine resistance stiffened. The Emperor Heraclius summoned a church assembly at Antioch, and the general opinion was that Byzantine disobedience to God was to blame for the Christian disaster. Many thought that the lost land would be regained after a suitable display of repentance, but when this did not happen some decided that it was the begining of the End of The World. Heraclius himself left the area more in sorrow than anger, supposedly with the words: 'Peace be with you, Syria - what a beautiful land you will be for the enemy.'

Yet the Emperor did not give up the fight; nor were his armies as paralysed as some historians suggest. They tried to establish new defences, and there was stiff fighting before a Muslim force took the important military centre of Chalcis. There was almost certainly a bitter struggle in the coastal mountains, but in general the Byzantines avoided major confrontations and negotiated a temporary truce for the years 637–8.

There were still pockets of resistance south of the Dead Sea, but this area, together with Palestine,

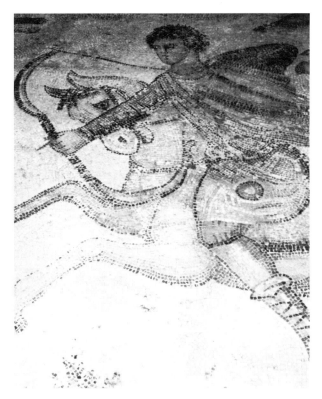

finally fell after the second conquest of Damascus. Jerusalem would only surrender to the Caliph 'Umar in person, finally opening its gates in 638. Caesarea Maritima was now the only Byzantine stronghold in Palestine. Its large garrison could be resupplied by sea, so the Muslims blockaded it by land until 640, when it and all the Byzantine-held ports except Tripoli fell to a series of violent assaults.

Though Syria was now, in Khalid Ibn al Walid's words, 'like a camel lying quietly', some Christian Arabs could not accept the new order. Among them was Jabala, the Ghassanid leader. In 638, with a large number of followers and their families, he crossed the frontier into Byzantine territory. He was never to forget his sunnier homeland and, as an educated Arab, inevitably put his feelings into verse:

'Oh would that my mother no son ever bore
Nor my name had in history found place.
How I yearn for the land of my fathers of yore,
Damascus, the home of my race.'

▲▼ *Byzantine mosaics from northern Syria tend to be of a finer quality than those in Jordan. This magnificent example* *showing members of the military élite hunting dates from the late 6th or early 7th century and was found in Antioch.* *Below shows a horseman thrusting with a spear. Above left another horseman shoots with a typical early Byzantine* *composite bow. (Worcester Art Museum, Massachusetts; author's photograph)*

AFTERMATH
AND RECKONING

The battle of Yarmuk has not received the attention it deserves, supposedly 'serious' scholars minimizing the military aspects of Byzantium's catastrophic defeat. This has not been helped by a persistent Western inability to take the early Muslim Arabs seriously in military terms. As a result, the crass excuses made by the Byzantines themselves have often been accepted by uncritical Western historians.

Performance of the Byzantine Army

Early Byzantine writers tried hard to shift the blame away from Heraclius, pointing to the Emperor's illness, a supposed mutiny by Armenian troops and a mythical dust storm. Heraclius was, in fact, far from the scene of battle and could only have interfered in general terms. The Caliph 'Umar, of course, similarly supervised operations from a distance. Later Byzantine writers were inclined to blame Heraclius, largely because of his unorthodox efforts to unite the various Christian churches.

The only truly disaffected groups in Syria were the Jews and Samaritans, who rarely served as soldiers. The Greek Byzantines also never fully trusted their Christian Arab auxiliaries. A more serious problem was the Byzantine shortage of money to pay its army and to maintain the friendship of neighbouring tribes. This failure almost certainly undermined discipline before the battle of Yarmuk. Byzantine forces in Palestine and Syria, though outnumbering the Muslim Arab invaders, were able to concentrate their forces and achieve a numerical advantage only on the battlefield at Yarmuk. Their subsequent defeat may have resulted from lack of coordination between commanders and friction between Armenians and Greeks. Yet the Byzantines clearly failed to make

▶ *The most mysterious Armenian carved relief of this period is in the ruined monastery of Surb Bartolomeos, now called Albak, east of Lake Van in Turkey. It shows a cavalryman, with a large Persian-style crest on his helmet, armed with a lance that he uses in the medieval couched manner, and a large archer's quiver on his right hip. He is overthrowing a horse archer, who clearly has stirrups. (in situ, monastery of Surb Bartolomeos/ Albak, Turkey; photograph via Centre d'Etudes et Documentation sur 'Art Chretien Oriental, Etampes)*

effective use of terrain – since this area was at the centre of Ghassanid territory, one can only assume that Jabala the Ghassanid's advice was ignored. The Byzantines also failed in their traditional tactic of subverting the enemy leadership, presumably as a result of the Muslim Arabs' new Faith.

Yarmuk is unusual because the Byzantine high command actually committed itself to a decisive battle, probably abandoning their traditional caution because they were so confident of victory. This could also explain the depths of despair that engulfed the army once the battle was lost, and the lack of a fall-back position.

Both sides used sophisticated tactics during the Yarmuk campaign, those of the Byzantines fully within their known military heritage. Where fortified cities were concerned, the length of resistance depended upon the condition of the walls, the morale of a garrison, the character of a commander, or the availability of food and water. Yet most towns only put up a token resistance to obtain decent surrender terms. In fact Syria was lost less because of Yarmuk than as a result of the urban population failing to resist in the way they had

previously resisted Persian invaders. In much of the countryside, ordinary people may well have felt that they were exchanging one set of Arab rulers for another: Ghassanids for Muslims.

For the Byzantine Empire as a whole the reign of Heraclius proved to be one of ephemeral victories and real defeats. Traditional Byzantine search-and-destroy tactics had failed, and new ones had to be explored. Over the next century these were developed into the defensive guerrilla strategy of 'Shadowing Warfare' in which raiders or invaders were harassed and ambushed rather than confronted in a major battle.

Performance of the Muslim Army

The Muslim invasion of Syria was not an irresistable mass movement of tribes. It was a carefully planned, coordinated and organized series of military operations using strategy well able to deal with Byzantine defensive measures. Muslim Arab tactics of penetration by several self-sufficient armies eliminated the traditional distinction between 'front' and 'rear', the Byzantine defending

▶ Coptic Egyptian 'folk art' is notoriously difficult to date, and this fragment of a painted vase is sometimes thought to have been made between the 2nd and 6th centuries. Certain aspects of the foot soldier's kit might, however, suggest the 6th to 9th centuries. (Benaki Mus., inv. 13953, Athens; author's photograph)

forces being defeated piecemeal. Muslim commanders clearly understood the military traditions of their enemy, while the Byzantines apparently did not understand the methods of the Muslims.

Khalid Ibn al Walid's famous march from Iraq to Syria showed how effectively the Muslims controlled the intervening desert steppes, home to many warlike tribes. It also demonstrated a high degree of control from the Caliph's capital at Madina. In battle the Muslim Arabs made excellent use of terrain, and they never blundered into battle unawares. Their willingness to attack at the hottest

part of the day and ability to remain effective with less drinking water than their enemies must have helped, though it would hardly have changed the military balance. The Arabs also cultivated a reputation for ferocity in warfare, which may have had a morale impact on the enemy, though this was based on isolated and rarely proven acts of savagery. Chroniclers of both sides also mentioned the ferocity of Arab women in battles. Their active role would have come as no surprise to their menfolk, though it deeply shocked the more 'sexist' Byzantines.

On the other hand, it would be wrong to to suggest that dedication was universal on the Muslim side at Yarmuk. There were clearly some desertions. The Lakhm and Judham tribes, which were also present in the Byzantine army, also fought with little enthusiasm for either cause.

◀ A late 6th or early 7th century mosaic from Antioch shows a fallen huntsman – a soldier judging from his uniform *– with a single-edged sword and a large shield. (Worcester Art Museum, Massachusetts; author's photographs)*

THE BATTLEFIELDS TODAY

The Muslim armies that conquered Byzantine Syria ranged over modern Syria, Jordan, Lebanon, Israel, the occupied territories of Palestine and northern Saudia Arabia. Three of the battlefields and the main siege described in this book are easily accessible today, the only exception being the most important – namely the battlefield of Yarmuk, which straddles the United Nations monitored ceasefire line between Syria and the Israeli-occupied Golan Heights. The Israeli-held part of the battlefield, with the exception of a narrow frontier strip where visitors are likely to be flagged down by half-tracks, is open to visitors. So is territory east of a line linking the Syrian villages of Sa'asa, Nawa and Mazayrib. To visit the area between this line and the cease-fire line itself, special permission is required from both the Syrian authorities and the UN office in Damascus. This takes time to obtain and is even required by Syrian citizens not resident in the area.

Cross-country vehicles are not necessary, though sturdy rock-proof shoes are. Minor roads are adequate everywhere, though rather pot-holed on the Israeli-occupied Golan Heights. Good hotels are available in cities and in towns like Dara'ah, Irbid and Tiberius. Israel generally lacks the 'cheap and cheerful' *funduq* local accommodation found in all Arab towns, but there are hospitable if not cheap kibbutz settlements that provide rooms. Israel also has more youth hostels and camp sites.

Damascus is among the most interesting cities in the Middle East, and the epic Muslim conquest was only one episode in its astonishingly long history. Ajnadayn is, in contrast, an isolated place with little of interest other than the battlefield. The region is a sparsely populated part of Israel dedicated to re-afforestation, with a few old villages like Kefar Zekharya (ex-Palestinian Zakariya), new Israeli settlements such as Netiv and the abandoned ruins of Arab villages. Almost all the mosques and

tombs that once dotted the area have been destroyed or lie quietly crumbling in the sun.

Fihl, on the Jordanian side of the Jordan valley, is a remarkably dramatic spot, though visited by few tourists. Part of the ancient city of Pella (Fihl) has been excavated, including some early Islamic houses built before the place was devastated by a huge earthquake. Roads between Fihl and Irbid are good, if somewhat hair-raising in the dramatic scenery of northern Jordan, but a new road has been built down the Wadi Kufrinja to the Jordan Valley, which makes 'Ajlun slightly closer. For those who want adventure, a precipitous track also runs from the 'Ajlun-Dayr Abu Sa'id road to Fihl.

If all the paperwork can be obtained, discretion is taken with passport stamps, and the visitor is

▲ *These columns formed part of a large Byzantine church in Pella. The city itself, which included houses from the Islamic Umayyad period and a* Mamluk mosque, lay to the left. To the right, the steep Tal al Husn served as a citadel. (Author's photograph)

◄ *The site of the battle of Yarmuk is still a very sensitive military area lying on the UN-monitored cease-fire line between Syria and the Israeli-occupied Golan Heights. This picture was taken from an unmanned Israeli front-line fort, looking east. A line of trees in the distance marks the Wadi Ruqqad* before it cuts its way into a deep gorge. A bridge crosses the river amid these trees, just as it did at the time of the battle, and beyond it lies the village of 'Ayn Dhakar, which is still inhabited because it lies within Syrian controlled territory. (Author's photograph)

prepared to use Egypt as an intermediary stepping-stone, it is possible to visit both parts of the Yarmuk battlefield. But, at the time of writing, it is emphatically NOT possible to cross the UN supervised cease-fire line on the Golan plateau. When this piece of occupied territory is, one hopes, returned to Syria as part of a peace agreement, the picture will change – as it already has in the liberated though still devastated Syrian city of Qunaitra. The eastern part of the occupied Golan plateau is, however, a singularly desolate place. Wildlife abounds and gazelle are liable to bound in front of a visitor's car; but their presence indicates an absence of people. The Arab villages have been obliterated since 1967, together with most of the mosques, tombs and other Islamic shrines on the plateau. The Syrian side is not particularly scenic, but for a student of military history from 2,000 BC to the present day it remains one of the most fascinating places in the world.

▲ *Quite where the fleeing Byzantines fell to their deaths after the battle of Yarmuk is unknown, though the episode was appalling enough to be remembered for many generations. Those attempting to escape from the main Byzantine encampment at Yaqusah could have ended up here, on the bluffs facing the Jordanian spa village of al Hamma. (Author's photograph)*

CHRONOLOGY

There are still unanswered questions about the chronology of the Muslim Arab conquest of Syria. The following sequence is followed in this book:

611–14 Sassanian Persian invasion & conquest of Syria.

629 Sassanian occupying troops agree to withdraw from Syria & other Byzantine territory.

September 629 Pro-Byzantine Arab tribes defeat Muslims at Mu'ta.

630 Byzantines massacre Jews in Jerusalem & Galilee.

21 March 630 Byzantine Emperor Heraclius' pilgrimage to Jerusalem.

632 Death of the Prophet Muhammad.

Winter 633/4 Three Muslim forces invade Palestine & Jordan, capture Areopolis (Ma'an).

4 February 634 Muslims defeat Byzantines at Dathin.

March–April 634 Khalid Ibn al Walid crosses desert from Iraq to Syria.

24 April 634 Muslims defeat Ghassanids at Marj Rahit.

Late May 634 Khalid Ibn al Walid captures Busra.

30 July 634 Muslims defeat Byzantines at Ajnadayn.

August 634 Skirmishes at Yaqusah and/or (1st) Marj al Suffar.

23 August 634 Death of Caliph Abu Bakr.

January 635 Muslims defeat Byzantines at Pella (Fihl).

February 635 Byzantines fight Muslims to a draw at (2nd) Marj al Suffar.

March 635 Start of first siege of Damascus.

4 September 635 Muslims' first conquest of Damascus.

November 635 Muslims' first conquest of Emesa (Hims).

Spring 636 Muslims evacuate Emesa & Damascus, withdraw to Jabiya area.

May 636 Byzantine forces advance against Muslims.

July 636 Preliminary clashes near Jabiya.

15–20 August 636 Muslims defeat Byzantines at Yarmuk.

December 636 Second & final Muslim conquest of Damascus.

Spring–summer 636 Final Muslim conquest of Syria & Lebanon.

August–September 637 Ghazzah surrenders to Muslims.

September 637 Jerusalem offers to surrender to Muslims.

Late 637 Byzantine & Muslim authorities agree one year truce in northern Syria.

January 638 Jerusalem surrenders to Caliph 'Umar.

Late 638 Muslims capture rest of northern Syria including Antioch (Antakya).

639 Byzantine forces regroup in Anatolia (Turkey).

December 639 Muslims under 'Amr Ibn al As invade Egypt.

639–40 Plague in Syria.

640 Muslims conquer Palestinian, Lebanese & Syrian coasts.

11 February 641 Death of Emperor Heraclius.

A GUIDE TO FURTHER READING

AKRAM, A. I. *The Sword of Allah: Khalid bin al Waleed, his Life and Campaigns* (Karachi 1970); tends to accept the original sources uncritically but includes a great deal of colourful detail.

AUSSARESSES, F. *L'Armée Byzantine á la Fin du VIe Siècle* (Paris 1909).

AL BALADHURI, Abu'l 'Abbas Ahmad (trans. P. Hitti), *The Origins of the Islamic State* (New York 1916).

CAETANI, L. *Annali dell'Islam* (Milan 1905–26, reprint Hildesheim 1972); old but still best analysis of the battle of Yarmuk and the terrain.

DE GOEJE, M. J. *Memoire sur le Conquête de la Syrie* (Leiden 1900); wide-ranging traditional account of the campaigns.

DENNIS, G. T. *Three Byzantine Military Treatises* (Washington 1985).

FRIES, N. *Das Heereswesen der Araber zur Zeit der Omaijaden nach Tabari* (Tübingen 1921); best information about early Islamic military equipment and armies.

GLUBB, J. B. *The Great Arab Conquests* (London 1963); insights by a soldier who knew the area well, though the battle of Yarmuk is incorrecty located.

HALDON, J. F. *Byzantine Praetorians: An Administrative, Institutional and Social Survey of the Opsikion and Tagmata c.580-900* (Bonn 1984).

—*Byzantium in the Seventh Century: The Transformation of a Culture* (Cambridge 1990).

—*Recruitment and Conscription in the Byzantine Army c.550–950* (Vienna 1979).

— 'Some Aspects of Byzantine Military Technology from the Sixth to the Tenth Centuries', *Byzantine and Modern Greek Studies* I (Birmingham 1975).

HILL, D. R. 'The Role of the Camel and the Horse in the Early Arab Conquests', in *War, Technology and Society in the Middle East*, ed. V. J. Parry & M. E. Yapp (London 1975).

JANDORA, J. W. 'The Battle of Yarmuk: A Reconstruction', in *Journal of Asian History* XIX (1985).

KAEGI, W. E. *Byzantium and the Early Islamic Conquests* (Cambridge 1992); best recent study, also containing the most up-to-date bibliography.

KENNEDY, H. *The Prophet and the Age of the Caliphates: The Islamic Near East from the Sixth to the Eleventh Centuries* (London 1986).

KOLIAS, G. T. *Byzantinischen Waffen* (Vienna 1988).

MAYERSON, P. 'The First Muslim Attacks on Southern Palestine (AD 633–634),' *Transactions and Proceedings of the American Philological Association* XCV (1964).

McGRAW Donner, F. *The Early Islamic Conquests* (Princeton 1981); the most comprehensive and lucid modern account of the subject.

SHABAN, M. A. *Islamic History, AD 600-750; A New Interpretation* (Cambridge 1971).

STRATOS, A. N. *Byzantium in the Seventh Century*, 5 vols. (Amsterdam 1968–80).

TABARI, Abu Ja'far Muhammad (various translators, ed. I. Abbas and C. E. Bosworth), *The History of Al Tabari* (New York 1985 – in progress).

WARGAMING YARMUK

The Arab conquest of Syria works very well as a campaign, whether it is restricted to the 630s or extended to a longer period, perhaps covering the Muslim invasions of Egypt, Asia Minor and the first assault on Constantinople itself. The significance of the Yarmuk campaign can perhaps be best appreciated by covering a longer period; this emphasises the drastic consequences of the Byzantine defeat, with the frontier pushed back into Anatolia and the rapid growth of Arab naval power based on the dockyards of Alexandria. Perhaps the quickest and easiest way to a strategic game is to use the 'Matrix Game' pioneered by Chris Engle in the USA, and developed in England by Bob Cordery and others at *Wargames Developments*. See *The NUGGET: The Journal of Wargames Developments* for continuing discussion of the Matrix game concept.

Seated around a map of the Middle East, with counters or figures representing the rival armies, four or five players represent the key historical leaders while an umpire controls the game. Each player may make one 'argument' per turn: this consists of an 'action', e.g., "I force-march my army to Damascus", and a result, say, "My army takes the besieging forces by surprise". A player can advance up to three reasons why his action is successful. In this case he might say, "The forced march succeeds because (1) My troops know the area, (2) They are fit and rested, having remained in camp last turn, and (3) My army contains a high proportion of cavalry and light troops, unencumbered by heavy armour and equipment." The umpire assesses the strength of a player's argument, allowing a reasonable argument a (say) 50 per cent chance of success, reducing the odds for poor arguments and increasing them for particularly clever ones. If the player succeeds in the example given above, his forces would be given a favourable die-roll modifier if the battle is resolved on a board-game style combat table; if the action is wargamed with figures, the forced-marchers could be given a head-start across the table, or arrive on the enemy flank part-way into the game. The Matrix game produces a narrative of events – an alternative history – that is as convincing as the arguments of the players. Played well, it can present a fascinating view of what might have been. The flavour of the game is

always enhanced when players have personal objectives, not always known by their own side, let alone the enemy. In the case of Yarmuk, we have several Byzantine commanders with obvious individual goals as well as various tribal leaders whose sole idea is to emerge on the winning side! This is perhaps the best way to represent the divisions within the Byzantine camp, leaving the Arab side to concentrate on purely military objectives.

If the free-wheeling novelty of the Matrix game is not to your taste, then the campaign works equally well as a more conventional boardgame. That old favourite, Albert S. Nofi's *Imperium Romanum II* (West End Games, 1985) charts the fortunes of the Roman Empire from the fall of the Republic to the wars of the 6th century. It ends with the reign of Justinian and the defeat of the Goths in Italy – but why stop there? The system works equally well for the campaigns of Heraclius and the subsequent disaster in Syria. As we have seen, the Arab armies enjoy better leadership, their generals deserving +1 or +2 ratings, while the Byzantines are mostly +0. (Under the *Imperium Romanum* rules, zero-rated generals have little ability to react to enemy movement; better commanders can move out of the normal sequence of play). The Arabs have an obvious advantage in 'Combat Efficiency Rating', probably deserving the 'A' rating, while the Byzantine army is divided between 'B' type regulars and 'C' rated auxiliaries. You will need to devise a new chart for this later period, bearing in mind that the Empire's resources are sadly depleted by the long war with Persia. The Byzantines' tax base will be low, and there should be limits on the quantity of heavy cavalry the Empire can assemble. Hence, to outnumber the Arabs, it will be necessary to rely on locally raised light troops.

Imperium Romanum emphasises the importance of logistics. In the early medieval period, poorly maintained roads and the inadequacies of horse-drawn transport severely restricted commanders' freedom of action. It was difficult to supply a large field army away from the coast or a major city, and especially so in the arid hill country where the armies finally clashed in 636. Note how both armies remained closely tied to fortified camps. The Arabs may have been more mobile when operating as dispersed groups of raiders, but they faced the same problems supplying their troops when they were concentrated. Wargamers are notorious for disregarding logistics in campaigns and on the table-top: but a Yarmuk campaign that ignored the armies' supply problems would bear little resemblance to historic events.

The Global View

Maps illustrating the Arab conquests of the seventh century give a very misleading idea if they are centred on the Mediterranean. Having achieved victory in Syria, 'Umar switched direction and dispatched reinforcements to Persia for the next campaigning season. Fourteen months after Yarmuk, the Arabs shattered Sassanian power in the three-day battle at Qadisiya. Within thirty years of Yarmuk, Arab armies had passed through Egypt and Libya to reach Tripoli; but they had also overrun Kabul and were poised to enter India. By expanding the campaign to cover the great sweep of seventh-century conquest, you begin to see the campaign from the Arab point of view.

One aspect that should not be ignored, particularly in a strategic simulation of the campaign, is the influence of religion on the morale of the rival armies and peoples. This is perhaps obvious in the case of the Arabs, united by their new faith. Unlike many recent enemies of the Byzantine Empire, the Arabs could not be swayed by offers of gold. At Yarmuk, it was the Emperor's army, not the Arab invasion force, that was riven by dissent.

Despite the tragic role religion continues to play in human conflict, it is seldom included in wargames. However, it was certainly one additional factor that prevented the Muslim armies from expanding farther north from Syria: in Anatolia, the Arabs were among a largely Christian population that did not welcome their presence. Asia Minor would remain part of the Empire until the defeat at Manzikert. Some Byzantine sources regarded the disaster at Yarmuk as divine punishment. In a Matrix game, the Byzantines as well as the Arabs, should feel free to bolster their arguments with the blessings of their respective Gods. Of course, if you appeal for divine assistance but suffer a setback, the impact on your troops' morale might be catastrophic; no-one will go into battle for a general clearly out of favour with God.

Yarmuk as a Table-Top Battle

At first glance, wargaming Yarmuk as a straightforward table-top battle seems much harder than recreating the better documented ancient or medieval battles. The armies' orders of battle are obscure, and narratives of the action are sketchy. However, we do have a good idea of the terrain and a fair understanding of the strengths and weaknesses of the Byzantine and Arab armies.

Previous titles in this series have mentioned the rise (and fall?) of the Wargames Research Group ancient rules. From the mid-1970s until recently, the ancient and medieval wargaming was dominated by the WRG rules that covered all wars from the dawn of human kind until the battle of Bosworth. But the wargaming public has proved unexpectedly conservative, and further developments of the original rules met with some disapproval. The radical 7th edition proved too much for some gamers, and the rules have lost their former prominence. This is odd: as Sir Michael Howard once observed, "Those who do not change their minds in the course of a decade have probably stopped thinking altogether'. Surely one of the great attractions of wargaming is the constant search for new approaches to old problems. There is no such thing as a *definitive* set of wargames rules.

WRG's controversial 7th edition dispensed with much of the mathematical precision of the previous set, but Phil Barker and Richard Bodley Scott's *De Bellis Antiquitatis* went much further. This deceptively simple, and rather more convincing, approach to ancient warfare has since gone from strength to strength, and its mechanisms have been exported to other periods in the pages of the monthly wargaming magazines. *DBA* compels both armies to operate from a camp – entirely historical as far as Yarmuk goes. However, there are a few additions worth considering for a re-fight of the historic battle. Yarmuk was a very protracted affair, lasting six days in all. You could fight the battle as a series of *DBA* battles, returning some of the eliminated units to action for each successive day. Less reliable auxiliaries may not come back at all. The loss of an army's camp would be critical, allowing hardly any units to return to the fray and perhaps lowering the combat value of all surviving forces.

The Yarmuk campaign includes some extraordinary characters that deserve to be included, either to add colour to a strategic game, or in a role-playing game of their own. Matrix games can often produce some incredible arguments, but it will be hard to top the affair of 'Jonah the lover' or the gallantry of Zarrar's sister, Khaula Bint al Azwar. Indeed, the role of women in the Arab victory ought to be emphasised in the game, if only for its shock value.